REBEL GIRLS

REBEL GIRLS MAKE DESSERT

Kid-Tested Recipes You Can Make, Bake + Share!

DK

CONTENTS

7	Hi, Rebels!
9	The Sweet Stuff: How to Use This Book
10	Kitchen Basics
18	**COOKIES, BROWNIES, AND BARS**
68	**CAKES AND CUPCAKES**
120	**FRUIT DESSERTS**
142	**PASTRIES, PUDDINGS, AND PIES**
194	**FROZEN TREATS**
214	Acknowledgements
215	About Rebel Girls
218	Index

HI, REBELS!

Welcome to the second Rebel Girls cookbook. We're so glad you're here! Are you on the hunt for a crowd-pleasing treat for a birthday or celebration? Looking to try something different after Sunday dinner? Do you need a quick recipe to satisfy your sweet tooth or maybe you and your bestie have all day and want to make something that will totally impress your family? No matter the reason, this book has lots of incredible options for you.

Whether you're craving something chocolatey or searching for a special way to use up the apples you picked this weekend, you're in the right place. The recipes in this book are as varied as they are delicious. You'll find cookies, cakes, puddings, bars, lollies, easy-to-make ice cream, and more. You'll also find desserts from around the world – honey-soaked cookies popular in Greece, jammy tarts from Guyana, a Brazilian carrot cake, and even a Lebanese-style fruit cocktail.

This book is also filled with handy information about making desserts. Whether you've been baking for years or you are just getting interested in whipping up treats for your family, you will be able to use and enjoy these recipes. Do you want to know the best way to turn a cake out of its tin or dust a dessert with icing sugar? The informative intro and step-by-step instructions will make tricky techniques simple and help boost your confidence in the kitchen.

Plus, you'll learn fun facts about chefs and women throughout history and hear from kids like you about the recipes they like best.

You'll also meet some of the Rebels currently ruling the food world. Molly Yeh, farmer and TV cooking show host, teaches you how easy it is to make your own sweet granola bars at home. Chrissy Tracey, forager and vegan chef, shows you an awesome way to use up leftover bananas with her Banana Split Bites. And award-winning pastry chef and author Abi Balingit shares a Mango Cream Pie recipe inspired by her favourite childhood snack. In this book, 14 talented chefs share stories, advice, and recipes – with you.

As you flip through these pages, we hope you are inspired to start chopping, whisking, mixing, baking, icing, and trying out new desserts. From gingerbread cookies and lemon bars to chocolate milkshakes and berry cobblers, the options are exciting and scrumptious. So, choose your dessert, wash your hands, and let's get cooking!

— THE REBEL GIRLS TEAM

THE SWEET STUFF: HOW TO USE THIS BOOK

GETTING STARTED

You've picked out a recipe and you're ready to start. But before you pull out ingredients or heat the oven, **read the entire recipe** from start to finish (and then maybe read it one more time)! This way you know what to expect, how involved the recipe is, and when you might need to ask a grown-up for support. Pay attention to the kitchen equipment you'll need to have on hand – it's in **pink** throughout each recipe.

Once you've read through the entire recipe, it's time to prep your ingredients. First things first: Tie back your hair if it's long and might get in your way and then wash your hands. Measure out ingredients using scales and measuring spoons. Wash and dry any fruits you'll be using before you chop them. Put each prepped ingredient in its own bowl to help stay organized.

Now it's time to make dessert! Follow the recipe steps, one at a time. If the recipe has step-by-step photos, check them before you begin and as you work. Be sure to ask a grown-up for help whenever you are using anything sharp (like a chef's knife or a food processor) or hot (like the oven).

And remember, if your dessert doesn't turn out quite the way you hoped, don't sweat it. Mistakes are a normal part of making dessert – and a great way to learn. Think about what you'd do differently next time. Plus, even if your cake or pie isn't perfect, we bet it still tastes great!

DECODING RECIPES

You'll see different symbols throughout this book. They will give you important information about each recipe. Here's what they mean.

!! This part of the recipe uses something sharp or really hot. Ask a grown-up for help before proceeding.

Recipe takes an hour or under to make.

Recipe uses a mixer or food processor.

Recipe doesn't require the use of the hob or oven.

 Recipe is vegan (doesn't include any animal products).

 Recipe can be customized just the way you like it.

 Recipe is gluten-free.

Kitchen Basics

These essential techniques show up in many recipes in this book ... and beyond! Practice them now, and you'll be ready to tackle just about any dessert recipe you come across.

How to Measure Wet and Dry Ingredients

Wet Ingredients

Use a **measuring jug** to measure wet ingredients, such as water or milk. Slowly add your liquid to the measuring jug until it reaches the correct line, such as 100 ml, 250 ml, or 500 ml. Bend down and get eye level with the measuring jug. Make sure the level of the liquid lines up with the measurement line.

Dry Ingredients

Use a **digital scale** to measure dry ingredients, such as flour and granulated sugar. Place the scale on a flat surface, and place your **mixing bowl** or **measuring jug** on the scale. Press the "zero" or "reset" button to remove the weight of the bowl or jug. Pour the desired ingredient into your bowl or jug.

MEASURING SPOONS

Use **measuring spoons** to measure small amounts of liquid and dry ingredients, such as lemon juice, vanilla extract, baking powder, and spices. A standard set of measuring spoons includes different spoons for 1 tablespoon, 1 teaspoon, ½ teaspoon, and ¼ teaspoon. Some sets also have ½ tablespoon and ⅛ teaspoon. After filling a measuring spoon, level off the dry ingredient with the flat back of a **butter knife**.

SPATULAS

There are many different kinds of spatulas and we've tried to specify as much as possible throughout the book. Since not all rubber spatulas are heat-resistant, we've called for silicone spatulas whenever you need to mix something hot. For transferring cookies or other goodies from a tray or sheet to a cooling rack or serving plate, we recommend any spatula that has a wide base.

HOW TO MELT BUTTER AND SOFTEN BUTTER AND CREAM CHEESE

Melting Butter on the Hob

Put the butter in a **small saucepan** and place the pan over low heat. Cook, swirling the saucepan occasionally, until the butter is melted. Turn off the hob and slide the saucepan to a cool burner. Leave to cool for 3 to 5 minutes.

Melting Butter in the Microwave

Use a **butter knife** to cut the butter into 1-tablespoon pieces. Place the butter in a **microwave-safe bowl** and cover the bowl with a **microwave-safe plate**. Microwave at 50 per cent power until the butter is melted, checking every 30 seconds. Leave to cool for 3 to 5 minutes.

Softening Butter or Cream Cheese

Place the amount of butter or cream cheese called for in the recipe on a worktop to soften 30 minutes to 1 hour before needed. It might need more time in the winter or less in the summer. It all depends on how warm your kitchen is. The butter or cream cheese is ready if it dents easily when pressed with a fingertip but still holds its shape.

HOW TO BRING EGGS, MILK, AND BUTTER TO ROOM TEMPERATURE

Take out the amount of the ingredient you will need 30 minutes to 1 hour before you want to start making your dessert. Place it on a worktop away from any super-warm spots in the kitchen (like the oven or in direct sun) or anywhere it might get knocked over. For eggs, make sure to place them in a **small bowl** so that they don't roll off the worktop!

HOW TO DO A TOOTHPICK TEST

‼ A toothpick test helps tell you if a cake or bar is done baking. Use **oven gloves** to remove the tin from the oven and place it on the hob. Take a **toothpick** and insert the pointy end into the centre of the dessert, making sure to go three-fourths of the way down into the bake. Slowly pull the toothpick back out.

If the toothpick is wet or has some batter clinging to it, return the tin to the oven for a few more minutes before repeating the test with another toothpick.

If the toothpick has some crumbs on it or comes out clean, turn off the oven and set the tin aside to cool.

HOW TO ZEST AND JUICE CITRUS FRUITS

TO ZEST

Zest comes from the colourful peel on lemons, limes, oranges, and other citrus fruits. To remove it, gently rub the fruit back and forth on a **fine grater** (sometimes called a Microplane, after the popular brand). Keep turning the fruit so you remove just the colourful skin, not the white layer underneath. Fine graters can be pretty sharp, so handle carefully. On average, one medium lemon will give you 1 tablespoon of zest.

‼ TO JUICE

On a **chopping board**, use a **chef's knife** to cut the fruit in half the short way. Place one half in a **citrus juicer**. Hold the juicer over a **small bowl** and squeeze, releasing the juice into the bowl. Repeat as needed to get the amount of juice for the recipe. On average, one medium lemon will give you 3 tablespoons of juice.

HOW TO MAKE A SINGLE FOIL OR PARCHMENT SLING

1

Have ready a piece of **aluminium foil** or **parchment paper** that is at least as wide as your **baking tin** in one direction and several centimetres longer in the other direction. Set the baking tin next to the foil or parchment and fold the sides of the foil or parchment towards the centre so the foil or parchment strip is the same width as the tin.

2

Lay the folded foil or parchment strip, folded side up, in the tin, pressing it flat against the bottom and then up the sides on two ends. It should extend above the sides by about 2.5 cm (1 in).

3

Crease the extra foil or parchment hanging over the sides along the edge of the tin. When baked and cooled, you can use these edges as "handles" to lift your creation neatly out of the tin.

KITCHEN BASICS

HOW TO LINE THE BOTTOM OF A CAKE TIN WITH PARCHMENT

1

Have ready a piece of **parchment paper** that is slightly bigger than the circumference of the **cake tin** and place the tin in the middle of the parchment.

2

Using a **pencil** or **pen**, trace the outside of the tin on the parchment.

3

Using **scissors**, cut out the shape.

4

Place the piece of parchment in the bottom of the tin. Discard the scraps of parchment.

HOW TO TURN A CAKE OUT OF A TIN

!! 1

The tin can sometimes still be warm when it's time to turn a cake out. If it is, make sure to wear oven gloves. Use a **butter knife** to gently loosen the sides of the cake from the tin.

2

Lay a **clean tea towel** over the top of the cake and gently place your nondominant hand on top of the towel. Slip an **oven glove** onto your dominant hand, lift the cake tin, and then flip the tin upside down, letting the cake fall onto the towel. Lift away the tin.

3

Set the cake tin aside and carefully peel off the parchment paper (if using) from the bottom of the cake.

4

Gently flip the cake so it's bottom side down and place it on a **cooling rack** or **plate**.

KITCHEN BASICS

HOW TO DUST DESSERTS WITH ICING SUGAR OR COCOA POWDER

1

Set a **fine-mesh sieve** over a **small bowl**. Add 1 to 2 teaspoons icing sugar or cocoa powder to the sieve.

2

Hold the sieve over your dessert. Gently tap the side of the sieve to dust with sugar or cocoa.

HOW TO MAKE WHIPPED CREAM

1

Chill the bowl and the **whisk attachment** of a **stand mixer** or a **large bowl** and the **whisks** of a **handheld mixer**. Add 250 ml double cream, 1 tablespoon icing sugar, and ½ teaspoon vanilla extract to the bowl. Whip the cream on medium-low speed until foamy bubbles form, about 1 minute.

2

Increase the speed to high and whip until the cream is thick and you can see ripples in it, 1 to 3 minutes. (If the cream is splattering out of the bowl, drape a **clean tea towel** over the mixer and bowl, or just the bowl if using a handheld mixer, to catch the drops.)

3

Stop the mixer. To check for soft peaks, lift the whisk (or beaters) out of the cream to see if it makes peaks that stand up on their own, with just a little droop at the top. If not, keep whipping and check again in 15 to 30 seconds. For stiff peaks, keep beating until the peaks stand up on their own without any drooping. Be careful not to overwhip the cream. If it turns grainy, you'll have made butter!

KITCHEN BASICS

20 Chewy Sugar Cookies	46 Choose-Your-Own-Adventure Granola Bars
Chewy Citrus Sugar Cookies	by Chef Molly Yeh
Chewy Candy Sugar Cookies	49 Peanut Blossom Cookies
23 Melomakarona	Tahini Blossom Cookies
25 Shortbread	51 Hamantaschen
29 Raspberry Crumb Bars	56 Hot Cocoa Cookies
by Chef Deb Perelman	58 Salted Caramel Chocolate Brownie Bites
32 Gingerbread Cookies	Salted Chocolate-Filled Brownie Bites
35 Brown Butter Oatmeal Cookies	61 Homemade Oreos
41 Almond Butter-Miso Cookies with Chocolate Chunks	by Chef Joanne Chang
by Chef Aran Goyoaga	64 Cereal Treats Your Way
42 Lemon Bars	66 Brookies

BROWNIES, AND BARS

MAKES 24 COOKIES

CHEWY SUGAR COOKIES

INGREDIENTS

270 g plain flour

½ teaspoon bicarbonate of soda

½ teaspoon baking powder

½ teaspoon table salt

180 g unsalted butter, melted and cooled (see page 11)

60 ml vegetable oil

275 g plus 110 g granulated sugar, measured separately

1 large egg

2 teaspoons vanilla extract

These cookies get maximum chew from the addition of melted butter and vegetable oil. They are also the perfect blank canvas for creative flavours! Try mixing in citrus zest or pressing in sweets (see the variations on the opposite page), swapping out the vanilla extract for another flavoured extract, or adding a pinch of warm spices, such as cinnamon, nutmeg, or ginger.

1. Set an oven rack in the middle position and heat the oven to 180°C. Line **two baking trays** with **parchment paper**.

2. In a **medium bowl**, **whisk** together the flour, bicarbonate of soda, baking powder, and salt.

3. In a **large bowl**, whisk together the melted butter, oil, and 275 g of the sugar until smooth. Add the egg and vanilla and whisk until well mixed.

4. Add the flour mixture to the sugar mixture and use a **rubber spatula** to stir until no dry flour remains and a soft dough has formed.

5. Use a **tablespoon** to scoop 12 heaped portions of dough onto one of the parchment-lined baking trays. Use your hands to roll each dough portion into a ball.

6. Place the remaining 110 g sugar in a **small shallow dish**. Working with a few dough balls at a time, roll them in the sugar until evenly coated, then space them 5 cm (2 in) apart on the baking tray.

7. Place the baking tray in the oven. Bake until the edges of the cookies are light golden brown and the tops are puffy and cracked, 12 to 14 minutes.

8. Meanwhile, repeat steps 5 and 6 to shape the remaining dough into balls, coat them with sugar, and arrange them on the second parchment-lined baking tray.

9. When the first batch of cookies is ready, use **oven gloves** to remove the baking tray from the oven and place it on the hob

FUN FOOD FACT

Juliette Gordon Low founded the Girl Scouts in the USA in 1912. Ten years later, the organization published a sugar cookie recipe in its magazine and encouraged troops to make and sell them to raise funds. Today, more than 200 million boxes of Girl Scout cookies are sold every year.

or a **cooling rack**. Let the cookies cool completely on the baking tray before serving, about 30 minutes.

10 Meanwhile, repeat steps 7 and 9 to bake the second batch of cookies. Alternatively, cover the second baking tray with **cling film** and freeze until the shaped cookies are solid, at least 2 hours. Once frozen, transfer the cookie dough portions to a **sealable plastic freezer bag** or other **airtight container** and freeze for up to 1 month. When you're ready to bake, heat the oven to 180°C, arrange the frozen cookies on a parchment-lined baking tray, and bake for 15 to 17 minutes.

CHEWY CITRUS SUGAR COOKIES

Add 1 teaspoon grated lemon, lime, or orange zest (see page 12) to the bowl with the melted butter and sugar in step 3.

CHEWY CANDY SUGAR COOKIES

After rolling the cookies in sugar in step 6 and arranging them on the baking sheet, press a few sweets, such as M&M'S, Reese's Pieces, or bits of a broken-up chocolate bar, into the top of each cookie.

YOU'RE THE CHEF!
"Melomakarona are amazing! The flavour of this cookie is so complex and beautiful. I love how the orange adds the perfect pop of flavour. Also, it was super easy to make!" —Madeline, 12

MELOMAKARONA

MAKES 20 COOKIES

Melomakarona are one of the most popular treats in Greece during the Christmas holidays. The word *melomakarona* is a combination of the word *meli*, which means "honey" in Greek, and the word *makarona*, which comes from the ancient Greek word *makaria* and means "blessed". The dough is flavoured with orange and cinnamon and then the cookies are soaked in a honey syrup after baking to make them extra moist and delicious. Using some semolina flour helps keep these cookies tender (and able to absorb the honey syrup), but if you don't have it, you can use an extra 30 g plain flour instead.

1. **For the syrup and topping:** In a **medium saucepan**, combine the honey, 175 ml water, 110 g sugar, and cinnamon stick (if using).

2. Place the saucepan on the hob over medium heat and cook, stirring occasionally with a **wooden spoon**, until the mixture comes to a simmer (small bubbles appear all over the surface) and the sugar dissolves, 5 to 7 minutes. Turn off the hob, slide the saucepan to a cool part of the hob, and let cool.

3. While the syrup is cooling, add the walnuts to a **sealable plastic bag**, press out all of the air, and seal the bag. Lay the bag flat on a worktop and use a **rolling pin** to pound the walnuts gently into very small bits. Set aside for later.

4. **For the cookies:** Set an oven rack in the middle position and heat the oven to 180°C. Line a **baking tray** with **parchment paper**.

5. In a **medium bowl**, **whisk** together the plain flour, semolina flour, cinnamon, baking powder, bicarbonate of soda, salt, and cloves.

6. In a **large bowl**, whisk together the oil, 110 g sugar, 60 ml water, and orange zest and juice.

7. Add the flour mixture to the oil mixture and use a **rubber spatula** to stir until no dry flour remains and a soft dough has formed.

8. Use a **tablespoon** to scoop 20 heaped portions of dough onto the parchment-lined baking tray. Make sure they are not touching one another.

INGREDIENTS

Syrup and Topping

350 g honey

175 ml water

110 g granulated sugar

1 cinnamon stick (optional)

55 g walnuts

Cookies

280 g plain flour

30 g semolina flour

1 teaspoon ground cinnamon

¾ teaspoon baking powder

½ teaspoon bicarbonate of soda

½ teaspoon table salt

¼ teaspoon ground cloves

120 ml olive oil

110 g granulated sugar

60 ml water

1 tablespoon grated orange zest (see page 12)

60 ml fresh orange juice (see page 12)

CONTINUED

COOKIES, BROWNIES, AND BARS

MELOMAKARONA
CONTINUED

9 Use your hands to roll the dough portions into oval shapes (like little eggs!), then space them evenly apart on the baking tray. Use a **fork** to prick three rows of holes in each cookie.

10 Place the baking tray in the oven. Bake until the cookies are puffed, cracked on top, and light golden brown, 25 to 28 minutes.

!! 11 Use **oven gloves** to remove the baking tray from the oven and place it on the hob or a **cooling rack**. Let the cookies cool on the baking tray for 5 minutes.

12 While the cookies are cooling, measure out 60 ml of the cooled honey syrup and place it in a **small bowl**. Add the crushed walnuts and use a **spoon** to stir to combine.

!! 13 Use a **spatula** to transfer a few warm cookies to the cooled syrup in the saucepan (be careful, as the baking tray will still be hot!). Let the cookies soak for 1 minute, then use a **slotted spoon** to flip each cookie over. Soak for 1 more minute, then use the slotted spoon to transfer the soaked cookies to a **serving platter**. Repeat with the remaining cookies.

14 Spoon a little bit of the walnut topping onto each cookie on the platter. Serve.

📣 FUN FOOD FACT

Bees buzz around from flower to flower collecting nectar so they can make honey. The ancient Greeks used honey as a delightful food and a helpful medicine. They associated honeybees with Artemis, the goddess of wild animals and the hunt. The priestesses in her temple were even referred to as "bees".

SHORTBREAD

MAKES 24 BISCUITS

Shortbread isn't bread at all but a biscuit. In this context, the word *short* means the texture is crumbly, while the word *bread* comes from the medieval term *biscuit bread*, which was made from leftover bread dough that was dried out in a low oven, similar to how we make cookies today. Traditional Scottish shortbread crumbles and melts in your mouth when you eat it. Cutting the shortbread while it's still warm makes it much easier to get clean lines for your cookies. If the slab has cooled completely before cutting, use a serrated bread knife instead of a chef's knife to cut it.

INGREDIENTS

Vegetable oil spray

190 g plain flour

75 g granulated sugar

½ teaspoon table salt

180 g unsalted butter, cut into 1 cm (½ in) cubes and chilled

1   Set an oven rack in the middle position and heat the oven to 170°C. Spray the inside of an **20 cm (8 in) square metal baking tin** with vegetable oil spray. Fit the baking tin with a **parchment paper** sling (see page 13).

2   Add the flour, sugar, and salt to a **food processor** and lock the lid into place. Pulse until well mixed, about three 1-second pulses.

3   Remove the processor lid and add the butter cubes. Lock the lid back into place and pulse until the butter has broken down into fine crumbs, eight to ten 1-second pulses. Then process the mixture until the dough comes together in clumps, about 1 minute. Stop the food processor.

!! 4   Remove the processor lid and carefully remove the processor blade. Use your hands to break the dough into pieces, then scatter the pieces evenly onto the bottom of the parchment-lined baking tin.

5   Lay a piece of **cling film** over the dough. Use your hands on top of the cling film to smoosh, spread, and press the dough into a flat, even layer in the bottom of the tin. If you want it extra flat, press the dough with the bottom of a **dry mug or glass** after pressing it into an even layer with your hands.

6   Use a **fork** to pierce holes all over the dough. (You can make lines or a fun design of your choice!)

CONTINUED

SHORTBREAD
CONTINUED

📣 FUN FOOD FACT

Many people say that Mary, Queen of Scots, invented shortbread. That's probably not true, but she sure did love to eat it! Back in her day, shortbread was flavoured with caraway seeds. Today, you are more likely to find caraway seeds in rye bread and sauerkraut.

7. Place the baking tin in the oven. Bake until the shortbread is pale golden brown all over with more deeply browned edges, 35 to 40 minutes.

⚠️ 8. Use **oven gloves** to remove the baking tin from the oven and place it on the hob or a **cooling rack**. Let the shortbread cool for 10 minutes.

9. Holding the edges of the parchment sling, carefully lift the shortbread out of the tin and onto a **chopping board**. The tin will still be warm and the shortbread will be soft, so try not to allow the shortbread to bend too much. If it cracks from bending, you can lightly press it back together on the chopping board.

10. Use a **chef's knife** to cut the warm slab of shortbread into thirds in one direction. Then cut the slab into eighths in the other direction by first cutting the whole slab in half, then cutting each half in half, and finally cutting each of those halves in half. You'll end up with 24 rectangles (or "shortbread fingers").

11. Let the shortbread biscuits cool completely and set, about 30 minutes. Serve alongside a cup of tea for a traditional British snack.

MEET CHEF DEB PERELMAN

Deb worked a bunch of jobs before she found the right path for her: cooking and then writing about it. She worked in an ice cream shop, managed a record store, and reported on technology. For a while, she was an art therapist. But she knew she wanted to do something else. She wanted to tell stories. So she started a blog, *Smitten*, to tell tales about her life in New York and the ridiculous dates she was going on.

Then she met and fell in love with her husband. No more bad dates to write about! But she did have food. She enjoyed writing about the recipes she was trying in her small city kitchen — what worked, what didn't, which recipes needed more flavour. In 2006, her blog, *Smitten Kitchen*, was born.

Deb focused on sharing recipes that anyone can make — recipes without lots of hard-to-find ingredients or equipment found only in restaurants. She wrote about her love of fritters, how to keep meatballs from falling apart, why cookies covered in sprinkles are better than cookies that aren't, and so much more.

She describes her cooking style as "classics stepped up in taste, ease, and reliability". Deb doesn't believe there are bad cooks in the world, just bad recipes. So she strives to write recipes that all people can follow, celebrate, and enjoy.

Deb's father taught her to love cream cheese and jam sandwiches. They taste just like cheesecake!

RASPBERRY CRUMB BARS

MAKES 12 BARS

"Here's a delicious raspberry crumb bar that's a cinch to make: tender, buttery, lemon-scented streusel for the base and topping and a sweet-tart mash of fresh or frozen raspberries and raspberry jam for the filling. Store any leftover bars in an airtight container in the fridge to keep them from softening." –Deb Perelman

INGREDIENTS

Crust and Topping

280 g plus 30 g plain flour, measured separately

½ teaspoon baking powder

¼ teaspoon table salt

150 g granulated sugar

Grated zest of 1 lemon (see page 12)

240 g unsalted butter, cut into 2.5 cm (1 in) cubes

Filling

125 g fresh or frozen raspberries

210 g raspberry jam

1. Set an oven rack in the middle position and heat the oven to 190°C. Fit an 20 cm (8 in) square metal baking tin with a parchment paper sling (see page 13).

2. **For the crust:** Add 280 g of flour, the baking powder, salt, sugar, and lemon zest to a food processor and lock the lid into place. Pulse until well mixed, about three 1-second pulses.

3. Remove the processor lid and add the butter cubes. Lock the lid back into place and run the machine until the mixture forms large clumps. That's right, just keep running it. It might take 30 seconds to 1 minute for the mixture to come together, but it will. If it is not mixing evenly, stop the processor, remove the lid, and use a rubber spatula to scrape down the sides of the bowl. Then lock the lid back into place and run the processor until the mixture comes together.

4. Remove the processor lid, and while keeping the processor blade in, carefully transfer half of the dough to the parchment-lined baking tin. Use the sides of a dry mug or glass to press the dough evenly across the bottom and 5 mm (¼ in) up the sides of the pan. Place the baking tin in the oven. Bake until the crust is golden at the edges, 15 to 20 minutes.

5. Use oven gloves to remove the tin from the oven and place it on the hob or a cooling rack. Let cool for 5 minutes, leaving the oven on.

6. **For the topping:** Add the remaining 30 g flour to the dough remaining in the processor. Lock the lid into place and pulse until the mixture is reduced to crumbs, eight to ten pulses. Carefully remove the processor lid and the processor blade.

CONTINUED

COOKIES, BROWNIES, AND BARS

RASPBERRY CRUMB BARS
CONTINUED

7 **For the filling:** In a **medium bowl**, mash the raspberries with a **fork** until mostly crushed. Stir in the jam.

8 Spread the raspberry mixture over the baked crust layer, leaving a 5 mm (¼ in) border around the edges. Sprinkle the crumbs evenly over the top.

!! 9 Use oven gloves to return the tin to the oven. Bake until the crumbs are golden at the edges, 40 to 45 minutes.

!! 10 Use oven gloves to remove the tin from the oven and place it on the cooling rack. Let cool completely.

11 Holding the edges of the parchment sling, carefully lift the slab of bars out of the tin and onto a **chopping board**. Use a **chef's knife** to cut the slab into thirds in one direction then cut into fourths in the other direction. You'll end up with 12 medium rectangles. Serve.

> Deb says she's "very nitpicky about recipes — not about making them fussy but about making them work". She wants young chefs to know being picky is an asset, not a hindrance.

MAKES ABOUT 24 COOKIES

Gingerbread Cookies

INGREDIENTS

280 g plain flour

95 g dark brown sugar

1½ teaspoons ground cinnamon

¾ teaspoon ground ginger

½ teaspoon ground allspice

½ teaspoon bicarbonate of soda

¼ teaspoon table salt

90 g unsalted butter, melted and cooled (see page 11)

160 g golden syrup

2 tablespoons whole milk

Gingerbread cookies get their unique taste from molasses, a thick, syrup-like substance that is a by-product of making white sugar. Use golden syrup here instead of black treacle, which can make these cookies a little too bitter. A 7.5 cm (3 in) cookie cutter will get you around two dozen cookies, but feel free to use whatever size cutter you have handy.

1. Set an oven rack in the middle position and heat the oven to 180ºC. Line **baking trays** with **parchment paper**.

2. In a **large bowl**, **whisk** together the flour, brown sugar, cinnamon, ginger, allspice, bicarbonate of soda, and salt.

3. Add the melted butter, molasses, and milk to the bowl and use a **rubber spatula** to stir and press together all of the ingredients until a soft, crumbly dough forms and no dry flour remains.

4. Scrape the dough onto a clean worktop. Knead the dough until it comes together, about 30 seconds. Return the dough to the bowl and clean the worktop.

5. Lay a large sheet of parchment paper on the clean worktop. Place the dough in the centre of the sheet and use your hands to press it into a 18 cm (7 in) circle.

6. Lay a second large sheet of parchment paper on top of the dough. Use a **rolling pin** to roll the dough between the sheets of parchment into an 28 cm (11 in) circle about 5 mm (¼ in) thick (see page 153).

7. Peel off the top sheet of parchment and set it aside. Use a **7.5 cm (3 in) cookie cutter** to cut the dough into shapes. Use a **spatula** to transfer the cookies to one of the parchment-lined baking trays. You should have about 12 cookies.

8. Place the baking tray in the oven. Bake until the edges of the cookies are slightly puffy and just set around the edges, 9 to 11 minutes.

CONTINUED

YOU'RE THE CHEF!
"They were delicious and would be fun to make for the holidays!"
—Liliya, 12

GINGERBREAD COOKIES
CONTINUED

9. While the cookies are in the oven, gather the dough scraps, press them into a ball, and then press the ball into a circle. Lay the parchment sheet you set aside on top, then repeat the rolling and cutting steps to yield 12 more cookies. Use the spatula to transfer the cookies to the second parchment-lined baking tray. Discard any remaining dough scraps.

!! 10. Use **oven gloves** to remove the first baking tray from the oven and place it on the hob or a **cooling rack**. Let the cookies cool on the baking tray for 10 minutes, then use the spatula to transfer them to a **large serving plate**.

11. While the first batch of cookies is cooling, repeat steps 6 to 8 to bake the second batch of cookies.

12. Let all the cookies cool completely, about 30 minutes. Serve.

REBEL IN THE KITCHEN

Every year, a gingerbread house is displayed at the White House in Washington, DC. In 2015, Susan Morrison, the first woman White House executive pastry chef, built a dark chocolate-covered gingerbread house that weighed nearly 227 kg (500 pounds)!

BROWN BUTTER OATMEAL COOKIES

MAKES 16 COOKIES

INGREDIENTS

180 g unsalted butter, cut into 12 equal pieces

½ teaspoon ground cinnamon

Pinch of ground nutmeg

125 g plain flour

½ teaspoon table salt

½ teaspoon bicarbonate of soda

185 g dark brown sugar

1 large whole egg plus 1 large egg yolk (see page 37)

1 teaspoon vanilla extract

200 g old-fashioned rolled oats

30 g chopped pecans or walnuts (optional)

Rich, nutty brown butter is something you won't find in the supermarket. Luckily, it's easy to make at home. As you slowly heat butter, something magical starts to happen: the milk solids separate, sink, and begin to turn brown, and your kitchen starts to smell like you're toasting nuts, not melting butter! This is a fun way to turn butter into something that tastes totally different. The super-flavourful butter is extra good in oatmeal cookie dough, but you can use it in a lot of other cookie recipes too (hint, hint – try it in chocolate chip cookies for a fun twist).

1. Set an oven rack in the middle position and heat the oven to 190°C. Line **baking trays** with **parchment paper**.

2. Add the butter to a **25 cm (10 in) frying pan**. Melt the butter on the hob over medium-high heat. When the butter is melted, turn down the heat to medium-low.

3. Continue to heat the butter, stirring occasionally with a **silicone spatula**, until it smells nutty and the solids visible on the bottom of the pan turn golden brown, 6 to 8 minutes. The butter may spatter a little bit but stirring helps. If your butter spatters too much, you can turn the heat down to low, but it will take a bit longer for the butter to brown. Turn off the hob and slide the frying pan to a cool part of the hob. Stir in the cinnamon and nutmeg. Let the butter cool slightly.

4. Meanwhile, in a **medium bowl**, **whisk** together the flour, salt, and bicarbonate of soda.

5. In a **large bowl**, whisk together the brown butter mixture, brown sugar, whole egg, egg yolk, and vanilla until combined. Use the silicone spatula to stir in the oats, then add the flour mixture and nuts (if using) and continue to stir and press until well mixed and no dry flour remains.

CONTINUED

BROWN BUTTER OATMEAL COOKIES
CONTINUED

REBEL IN THE KITCHEN

Christina Tosi is an award-winning pastry chef and founder of the US-based dessert and bakery restaurant Milk Bar. Even though she's known for incredible desserts like Compost Cookies and Milk Bar Pie, she's a huge oatmeal cookie fan. She says her "hands-down, all-time" favourite dessert is her grandma's oatmeal cookie.

6. Use a large spoon to scoop eight 2-tablespoon portions of dough onto one of the parchment-lined baking trays. Use your hands to roll each dough portion into a ball, then space the balls about 5 cm (2 in) apart.

7. Place the first baking tray in the oven. Bake until the edges of the cookies are set and lightly browned (the centres will still be soft), 8 to 10 minutes.

!!8. Use oven gloves to remove the baking tray from the oven and place it on the hob or a cooling rack. Let the cookies cool on the baking tray for 10 minutes. While the first batch of cookies is cooling, repeat steps 6 and 7 to make the second batch of cookies.

9. Use a spatula to transfer the cookies to a large serving plate. Let them cool completely before serving, about 30 minutes.

HOW TO SEPARATE EGGS

1

Crack the egg into a **small bowl**.

2

Use your hand to gently lift the yolk out of the bowl and shake off the excess egg white, letting it run through your fingers. Transfer the yolk to a **second small bowl**.

3

If you need to separate more than one egg, repeat step 1 with a **third small bowl**. This way, if the egg yolk breaks, it won't contaminate the previously separated egg white.

4

Repeat step 2 and place the yolk in the second small bowl and the white in the first small bowl. Once you've separated the number of yolks and/or whites you need, wash your hands well with soap and warm water.

> Aran video-calls her parents in Spain every morning.

Aran can't remember a time before she was cooking. Her grandparents owned a bakery where her mother and all her mother's siblings worked. So Aran's been surrounded by bakers and pastry chefs since the day she was born. As a young girl, she remembers helping her grandmother with simple steps. She'd dip shortbread into chocolate or stir the pastry cream that her grandmother would use to fill brioche buns. To this day, the smells of cinnamon and vanilla can transport her back to her family's pastry shop.

By the time she was 10 (maybe even younger!), she was gutting and cleaning the fish her mum was cooking for dinner. As a teenager, she would cook Sunday lunches for the whole family.

At 24, she moved from the Basque country in northern Spain to the United States. She discovered she had a gluten intolerance, and that is when her adventures in gluten-free cooking began. With her pastry-making background, she already understood the science behind baking. But she still had a lot of exploring and experimenting to do, so she got right to it.

In 2008, she launched her blog, *Cannelle et Vanille* ("Cinnamon and Vanilla" in French). In it, she shares her stories, photos, and recipes. Aran describes her cooking style as "nourishing, textural, and simple". She has published three cookbooks and has more in the works.

> If Aran could host a dinner party with any woman from history, she'd invite gospel legend Mahalia Jackson and civil rights icon Rosa Parks. She says, "I would probably make them some Basque dish they'd likely never had before, like bacalao al pil pil or croquetas de jamón."

COOKIES, BROWNIES, AND BARS

Almond Butter-Miso Cookies
with Chocolate Chunks

MAKES 13 COOKIES

"These cookies straddle sweet and savoury. Before baking, let this dough chill in the fridge to hydrate, to ensure a crispy and gooey cookie. Look for white miso, also labeled 'shiro miso', in the chilled section of your supermarket. Not all miso is gluten-free, so check the label. To make this recipe vegan, add a flax egg instead by whisking together 1 tablespoon ground flaxseed and 2½ tablespoons hot water until blended. Let it sit until the mixture thickens to a jellylike consistency, about 5 minutes." —Aran Goyoaga

Ingredients

- 145 g unsalted butter or dairy-free butter, melted and cooled (see page 11)
- 185 g light brown sugar
- 90 g almond butter
- 2½ tablespoons white (shiro) miso
- 2 teaspoons vanilla bean paste or vanilla extract
- 1 large egg
- 155 g gluten-free oat flour
- 30 g tapioca starch or cornflour
- ½ teaspoon bicarbonate of soda
- 115 g 70 per cent cacao dark chocolate or any other dark chocolate, roughly chopped

1. Add the melted butter to a medium bowl and whisk in the brown sugar, almond butter, miso, and vanilla until smooth. Whisk in the egg until smooth.

2. In another medium bowl, stir together the oat flour, tapioca starch, and bicarbonate of soda. Add the flour mixture to the butter mixture and stir together using a wooden spoon until no dry flour remains and a soft dough has formed. Add the chocolate and stir until evenly distributed. Cover the bowl with cling film and chill in the fridge for at least 4 hours or preferably overnight.

3. Set one oven rack in the middle position and a second rack in the bottom position and heat the oven to 180°C. Line two baking trays with parchment paper.

4. For each cookie, use a large spoon to scoop 3-tablespoon portions of dough and use your hands to shape the dough into a ball. Place six balls of dough on one parchment-lined baking tray and seven balls on the other, spacing them 7.5 cm (3 in) apart. Bake the cookies until golden brown, 12 to 13 minutes.

!!5. Use oven gloves to remove the baking trays from the oven and place on the hob or cooling racks. Let the cookies cool on the baking trays for 10 minutes before using a spatula to transfer them to a serving plate. Enjoy warm or let them fully cool on the plate for about 30 minutes before eating. The cookies will keep in an airtight container at room temperature for up to 3 days.

MAKES 16 BARS

LEMON BARS

INGREDIENTS

Crust

Vegetable oil spray

190 g plain flour

85 g icing sugar

¾ teaspoon table salt

1 teaspoon grated lemon zest (see page 12)

180 g unsalted butter, melted and cooled (see page 11)

Filling

3 large whole eggs plus 1 large egg yolk (see page 37)

1 teaspoon grated lemon zest

110 ml fresh lemon juice (see page 12)

170 g icing sugar, plus more for dusting

3 tablespoons plain flour

These golden yellow bars are great to make year-round, but they are especially welcome in wintertime when everyone needs a little sunshine – and when lemons are in season! Be sure you have at least three lemons on hand for the juice and zest. Since you use the lemon zest in the crust and the filling, we recommend zesting all of the lemons into one bowl and measuring out the zest from there before cutting them for juice.

1. Set an oven rack in the middle position and heat the oven to 180°C. Lightly spray the inside of an **20 cm (8 in) square metal baking tin** with vegetable oil spray. Fit the baking tin with a **parchment paper** sling (see page 13). Lightly spray the parchment with vegetable oil spray.

2. **For the crust:** In a **large bowl**, **whisk** together the 190 g flour, 85 g icing sugar, the salt, and 1 teaspoon zest.

3. Add the melted butter and stir with a **rubber spatula** until combined. Transfer the mixture to the parchment-lined baking tin (don't wash the bowl!) and use the bottom of a **dry mug or glass cup** to press the mixture into an even layer.

4. Place the baking tin in the oven. Bake until the crust is golden brown, 19 to 24 minutes.

5. **While the crust is baking, make the filling:** Add the whole eggs, egg yolk, 1 teaspoon zest, lemon juice, 170 g icing sugar, and 3 tablespoons flour to the now-empty bowl and whisk until smooth.

!! 6. Use **oven gloves** to remove the baking tin from the oven and place it on the hob or a **cooling rack**. Let the crust cool for about 5 minutes.

!! 7. Carefully pour the filling over the warm crust. Use oven gloves to lift the tin and tap it lightly on a worktop to release any trapped air bubbles. Then use the oven gloves to return the baking tin to the oven. Bake until the filling is set and jiggles just a little when you gently shake the tin, 20 to 25 minutes.

!! 8. Use oven gloves to remove the baking tin from the oven and place it on the hob or the cooling rack. Let the lemon bars cool completely in the tin, about 1 hour.

9 Holding the edges of the parchment sling, carefully lift the bars out of the baking tin and onto a chopping board. Dust the bars with icing sugar (see page 16). Use a chef's knife to cut the slab of bars into fourths in one direction, then cut the slab into fourths in the other direction. You'll end up with 16 squares. Serve.

📢 FUN FOOD FACT

Although lemon juice is pale yellow, it dries clear. During World War I, spies used it to make invisible ink. In 1915, a British woman named Mabel Beatrice Elliott, who worked as a postal censor, grew suspicious of a certain letter. So she heated up the letter, which caused the invisible ink to turn dark brown. She used her knowledge of chemistry and her powers of observation to catch German spies!

Molly's advice to chefs in training? "Clean as you go. My mum used to say 'a messy kitchen is a happy kitchen,' which is charming and cute. It's true to an extent, but now I just cannot function if a spatula is dripping with batter and sitting on the worktop."

Molly's childhood is filled with fun food memories. She would sit on the kitchen floor as a kid, scooping blue and pink batter into cupcake tins with her mum and her sister. She enjoyed experimenting with her Easy-Bake Oven, but waiting for those little cakes to bake was agony! It felt like it took forever.

Going out for dim sum with her family in Chicago, Molly discovered a flavour that she has loved ever since: red bean paste! "I loved getting the red bean paste-filled sesame balls," she says. "They were so perfectly spherical and geometrically satisfying. So chewy and nutty. I love those little guys, and I loved sunny Sunday mornings sitting at a giant table of dumplings with my family."

Molly studied percussion at Juilliard and fell in love with food while living in New York City. She performed with orchestras around the world before moving to a farm on the North Dakota—Minnesota border, where she now lives with her farmer husband, her kids, and some very fluffy cats.

In her blog, her books, and her TV show *Girl Meets Farm*, Molly showcases her unique cooking style, which is inspired by a delightful mix of influences: her Chinese and Jewish roots, her husband's Scandinavian heritage, and the traditions of the American Midwest. She loves big, rustic, homestyle baked goods. And she says, "I love incorporating unexpected ingredients or techniques that tell a story."

Molly's dream dinner party would be full of fun food and big laughs. She would invite comedians Abbi Jacobson and Ilana Glazer and superstar figure skater Michelle Kwan. She'd serve up a hot dish and cookie salad (a pudding dessert topped with crushed cookies!).

COOKIES, BROWNIES, AND BARS

MAKES 16 BARS

CHOOSE-YOUR-OWN-ADVENTURE GRANOLA BARS

INGREDIENTS

400 g tin sweetened condensed dairy milk or sweetened condensed coconut milk

120 g unsweetened nut or seed butter (if using unsalted nut butter, add a couple of pinches of kosher salt)

300 g quick-cooking rolled oats

210 g mix-ins of your choice (such as sweets, dried fruit, and nuts)

"This is the perfect recipe to make when you feel like baking something easy and have some odds and ends lying around in your snack cupboard. Make the granola bar base (it's just three ingredients!) and then toss in those odds and ends to your heart's desire. The last few cookies from the box? Chop them up and toss them in. A handful of raisins? Sure! A spoonful of hemp or chia seeds that you're not sure you like but they seem cool and full of nutrients? Oh heck yeah. Stick to a random mix or follow a theme. Go wild with creativity – the world is your granola bar oyster. Some themes I love are s'mores (marshmallows, chocolate chips, and crushed graham crackers), trail mix (nuts, raisins, and candy-coated chocolates), and birthday cake (sprinkles and white chocolate chips)." –Molly Yeh

1. Set an oven rack in the middle position and heat the oven to 180°C. Fit an 20 cm (8 in) square metal baking tin with a parchment paper sling (see page 13).

2. In a large bowl, use a rubber spatula to stir together the condensed milk and nut or seed butter (and salt if using unsalted nut butter). Add the oats and most of the mix-ins, reserving a handful of mix-ins for the top, and stir to mix well.

3. Scrape the oat mixture into the parchment-lined baking tin and spread it out evenly, then press it flat with the rubber spatula. Press the remaining mix-ins into the top. Bake until lightly browned around the edges, about 25 minutes.

!! 4. Use oven gloves to remove the tin from the oven and place it on the hob or a cooling rack. Let cool in the tin for 15 minutes, then run a butter knife along the edges of the tin to release the bars. Holding the edges of the parchment sling, carefully lift the slab of bars out of the baking tin and onto another cooling rack. Let cool completely, about 1 hour.

5 Move the bars to a **chopping board**. Use a **chef's knife** to cut the whole slab in half in one direction. Then cut the slab into eighths in the other direction by first cutting the whole slab in half, then cutting each half in half, and finally cutting each of those halves in half. You'll end up with 16 bars. Store the bars in an **airtight container** at room temperature for a few days, in the fridge for up to 1 week, or in the freezer for up to 3 months.

Peanut Blossom Cookies

MAKES 24 COOKIES

INGREDIENTS

90 g plain flour

½ teaspoon bicarbonate of soda

¼ teaspoon table salt

140 g light brown sugar

120 g smooth peanut butter

1 large egg

30 g unsalted butter, melted and cooled (see page 11)

½ teaspoon vanilla extract

75 g granulated sugar

24 chocolates

You can use any flavour or style of chocolate you like for this recipe, including chocolate buttons. Chilling the dough balls in the fridge before baking helps them to keep their shape in the oven, making them the ideal size for placing the chocolate. You'll need to work quickly when these cookies come out of the oven, as they have to be warm and soft when you add the chocolate. Moving the cookies off the baking tray first makes this step safer. That way, you won't have to worry about grazing your arm or hands on the hot tray as you press in each chocolate.

1. Line a **baking tray** with **parchment paper**.

2. In a **medium bowl**, **whisk** together the flour, bicarbonate of soda, and salt.

3. In a **large bowl**, use a **rubber spatula** to stir together the brown sugar, peanut butter, egg, melted butter, and vanilla until well mixed.

4. Add the flour mixture to the brown sugar mixture and use the rubber spatula to stir until no dry flour remains and a soft dough has formed.

5. Use a **tablespoon** to scoop twenty-four 1-tablespoon portions of dough onto the parchment-lined baking tray. Use your hands to roll each dough portion into a ball.

6. Place the granulated sugar in a **small shallow dish**. Working with a few dough balls at a time, roll them in the sugar until evenly coated, then space them 2.5 cm (1 in) apart on the baking tray.

7. Place the baking tray in the fridge to chill the dough for 15 minutes. While the dough chills, set an oven rack in the middle position and heat the oven to 180°C.

CONTINUED

REBEL IN THE KITCHEN

In the 1950s, an Ohio grandmother named Freda Smith was whipping up a batch of peanut butter cookies for her grandsons. She thought they looked a bit boring, so she popped a chocolate kiss on top. She entered her cookies in a Pillsbury Bake-Off, and the peanut blossom cookie was born!

COOKIES, BROWNIES, AND BARS

PEANUT BLOSSOM COOKIES
CONTINUED

8 Remove the baking tray from the fridge and place it in the oven. Bake until the edges of the cookies are just set and the tops are puffy and beginning to crack, 10 to 12 minutes.

!! 9 Use **oven gloves** to remove the baking tray from the oven and place it on the hob or a **cooling rack**. Immediately use a **spatula** to carefully transfer the cookies to a **large serving platter** or **two large plates** (the baking tray will be very hot, and the cookies will be very soft).

10 While the cookies are still warm, gently press a chocolate into the centre of each cookie. Let the cookies cool completely, about 30 minutes. Serve.

TAHINI BLOSSOM COOKIES

Use tahini in place of the peanut butter (make sure to stir it well before measuring). Do not add the melted butter. Roll the dough balls in white sesame seeds instead of granulated sugar.

HAMANTASCHEN

MAKES 12 TO 16 COOKIES

Hamantaschen are filled, pastry-like cookies enjoyed during the Jewish holiday of Purim. Purim celebrates the triumph of Esther, a Jewish hero from the Bible, over the evil government minister Haman, who sought to persecute her people. The cookies are triangular to represent the three-cornered hat that was worn by Haman. To help these cookies keep their shape, the dough needs to chill twice. You can split this project across two days if you prefer, making and rolling out the dough on day one and cutting, shaping, and baking the cookies on day two.

Shaping hamantaschen takes some practice! If the dough is not firmly pinched together, the bubbling filling will sometimes push the sides of the cookies open. If some of your hamantaschen don't turn out as perfect triangles, don't worry. They'll still taste delicious! And with some practice, you'll be shaping them like a pro in no time.

INGREDIENTS

220 g plain flour, plus extra for dusting

¼ teaspoon table salt

120 g unsalted butter, softened (see page 11)

110 g granulated sugar

1 large egg

½ teaspoon vanilla extract

120 g apricot preserve or raspberry jam

1. In a **medium bowl**, **whisk** together the flour and salt.

2. Add the softened butter and sugar to the bowl of a **stand mixer** fitted with the **paddle attachment** or to a **large bowl** if using a **handheld mixer**. Beat the butter mixture on medium speed until light and fluffy, about 2 minutes. Stop the mixer.

3. Use a **rubber spatula** to scrape down the sides of the bowl and the paddle or beaters. Add the egg and vanilla. Beat on medium speed until well combined, about 1 minute. Stop the mixer.

4. Scrape down the sides of the bowl. Add half of the flour mixture. Beat on low speed until the flour is fully incorporated and there are no dry spots, about 30 seconds. Stop the mixer. Add the remaining flour mixture. Beat on low speed until no dry flour remains and the dough clumps together, about 1 minute. Stop the mixer. Remove the paddle or beaters and scrape any dough sticking to them into the bowl.

5. Sprinkle a clean worktop with a little flour. Scrape the dough onto the worktop and use your hands to gather it into a ball. Gently squish and knead the dough until it's smooth and uniform, about 15 seconds. Press the dough into a 15 cm (6 in) circle.

6. Lay a large sheet of **parchment paper** on the worktop and place the dough circle on the centre of the parchment. Lay a second large sheet of parchment paper on top of the dough.

CONTINUED

COOKIES, BROWNIES, AND BARS

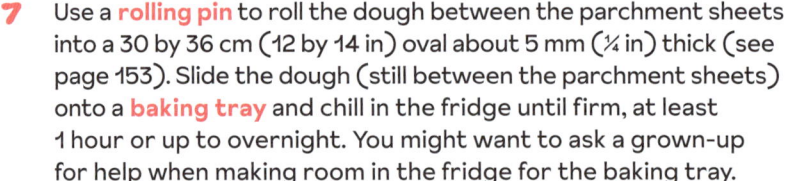

HAMANTASCHEN
CONTINUED

7 Use a **rolling pin** to roll the dough between the parchment sheets into a 30 by 36 cm (12 by 14 in) oval about 5 mm (¼ in) thick (see page 153). Slide the dough (still between the parchment sheets) onto a **baking tray** and chill in the fridge until firm, at least 1 hour or up to overnight. You might want to ask a grown-up for help when making room in the fridge for the baking tray.

8 Slide the chilled dough (still between the parchment sheets) off the baking tray onto the worktop. Line the baking tray with a fresh sheet of parchment paper (you'll use this for baking the cookies). Fill a **small bowl** with water and set it on the worktop.

9 Peel off the top sheet of parchment and set it aside. Use a **7.5 cm (3 in) round cookie cutter** to cut as many circles as possible from the dough (you should get 10 to 12).

10 Follow the photos on pages 54 and 55 to fill and shape your hamantaschen. (If the dough is very firm from chilling and cracks when folded, let it soften for 5 to 10 minutes on the worktop before continuing with shaping.)

11 Gather the dough scraps into a ball, knead gently just until smooth, and then press into a circle. Lay the parchment sheet you set aside on top and roll the dough into a circle or oval 5 mm (¼ in) thick. Cut out two to four more circles, fill and shape them, and add them to the baking tray.

12 Place the baking tray in the fridge and chill the cookies until firm, at least 30 minutes or up to 1 hour (the longer you chill the cookies, the better they will hold their shape when baking). About 20 minutes before you are ready to pull the baking tray from the fridge, set an oven rack in the middle position and heat the oven to 180°C.

13 Remove the baking tray from the fridge and place it in the oven. Bake until the filling is bubbling and the corners and edges of the cookies are just beginning to brown, 15 to 18 minutes.

!! 14 Use **oven gloves** to remove the baking tray from the oven and place it on the hob or a **cooling rack**. Let the cookies cool completely on the baking tray, about 30 minutes. Serve.

HOW TO FILL AND SHAPE HAMANTASCHEN

1

Working with one circle at a time, place 1 teaspoon jam in the centre of a dough circle. Dip your finger in the bowl of water and draw it around the edge of the circle to moisten.

YOU'RE THE CHEF!
"They taste really good! We like the combination of the cookie with the jam."
—Isabelle, 9, and Willa, 7

2

Pinch the top edge of the circle into a pointed shape, keeping the filling on the inside. (Don't pinch too hard, though! If the corners get very thin, they are more likely to burn in the oven.) Then use your fingers and thumbs to pinch the two bottom sides to form a triangle with walls that keep the filling in the middle.

3

Gently push the walls in towards the middle and pinch them together, leaving a small triangular window with the filling peeking through. Place the shaped cookie onto the parchment-lined baking tray. Repeat with the remaining dough circles and filling, spacing the cookies at least 2.5 cm (1 in) apart.

MAKES 12 COOKIES

HOT COCOA COOKIES

INGREDIENTS

Vegetable oil spray
90 g plain flour
3 tablespoons unsweetened Dutch-processed cocoa powder, plus more for sprinkling
¾ teaspoon baking powder
½ teaspoon table salt
135 g dark chocolate chips
30 g unsalted butter, cut into 1-tablespoon pieces
140 g light brown sugar
1 large egg
2 tablespoons milk
12 regular-sized marshmallows

Dutch-processed cocoa powder gives these cookies a deep chocolate flavour and a rich colour and texture. If you use natural cocoa powder, the cookies will be a bit drier, more crumbly, and lighter in colour. To get that toasty marshmallow on top, you need to bake these cookies on a rack set near the top of the oven so heat from the oven ceiling can reflect back onto them. Position your rack 10–15 cm (4–6 in) from the top of your oven. The cookies will puff up as they bake, so make sure the rack isn't so close that the marshmallows will hit the grill element or ceiling during baking.

1. Set an oven rack in the top position and heat the oven to 180°C. Line a baking tray with parchment paper and spray it with vegetable oil spray.

2. In a medium bowl, whisk together the flour, cocoa powder, baking powder, and salt.

3. In a large microwave-safe bowl, combine the chocolate chips and butter. Microwave at 50 per cent power until melted, 3 to 5 minutes. Stop the microwave once every minute and stir the mixture with a silicone spatula to see if it has melted. Use oven gloves to remove the bowl from the microwave and place it on the worktop.

4. Use the spatula to stir the melted chocolate and butter together until smooth. Add the brown sugar, egg, and milk to the melted chocolate mixture and whisk until smooth.

5. Add the flour mixture to the chocolate mixture and use the rubber spatula to stir until no dry flour remains and a soft, fudgy dough forms.

6. Use a tablespoon to scoop twelve 2-tablespoon portions of dough onto the greased parchment-lined baking sheet. (Use a small spoon to scoop out the dough from the measuring spoon, as it will be very sticky.) Let sit at room temperature for 10 minutes (this helps the cocoa to hydrate and the dough to firm up).

7. Use your hands to roll the dough portions into balls. (If the dough is still sticky, you can let it sit a little longer or lightly wet your hands with water when rolling.) Space the balls about 5 cm

(2 in) apart on the baking tray. Gently flatten each dough ball a little with your fingers.

8. Place the baking tray in the oven. Bake until the cookies are puffed and beginning to crack but still very soft, about 7 minutes.

!! 9. Use **oven gloves** to remove the baking tray from the oven and place it on the hob or a **cooling rack**. Working quickly while the cookies are still hot, gently press a marshmallow, flat side down, into the middle of each cookie. Be careful, as the baking tray will be very hot!

!! 10. Use oven gloves to return the baking tray to the oven. Continue to bake until the edges of the cookies are set and the marshmallows are puffed and beginning to brown, 6 to 9 minutes.

!! 11. Use oven gloves to remove the baking tray from the oven and place it on the hob or a cooling rack. Let the cookies cool on the baking tray for at least 15 minutes to set fully. (The marshmallows will melt and deflate a little bit — that's OK!)

12. Use a **fine-mesh sieve** to sprinkle each cookie with a little cocoa powder (see page 16). Serve warm or at room temperature.

YOU'RE THE CHEF!
"The cookies are very delicious. I especially like how gooey the marshmallow is and how chocolatey the cookie is. It really tastes like if hot cocoa were a cookie!" –Neva, 12

MAKES 12 BROWNIE BITES

SALTED CARAMEL CHOCOLATE BROWNIE BITES

INGREDIENTS

Vegetable oil spray

60 g dark chocolate chips

40 g unsweetened Dutch-processed cocoa powder

120 ml boiling water

365 g granulated sugar

120 ml vegetable oil

2 large eggs

2 teaspoons vanilla extract

190 g plain flour

¾ teaspoon table salt

12 soft caramels, wrappers removed

1½ teaspoons flaky sea salt

These brownie bites have crispy edges and a gooey centre. You can use natural cocoa powder in this recipe if you don't have Dutch-processed cocoa handy. The big crystals of flaky sea salt from brands like Maldon give these treats nice pops of salty flavour to balance the sweet caramel filling. If you don't have flaky salt, you can substitute coarse kosher salt. Don't use table salt, as it is too fine to use as a topping. Make sure to use nonstick parchment cupcake liners and spray them and the tin with vegetable oil spray so the brownie bites don't stick to the tin.

1. Set an oven rack in the middle position and heat the oven to 180°C. Line a 12-hole muffin tin with nonstick parchment cupcake liners and spray the inside of each liner and the top of the tin generously with vegetable oil spray.

!! 2. In a large heatproof bowl, combine the chocolate chips and cocoa powder. Pour the boiling water over the mixture and let it sit until the chocolate chips melt, about 5 minutes. Whisk together until the chocolate is fully melted and the mixture is smooth.

3. Add the sugar, oil, eggs, and vanilla and whisk until combined. Add the flour and table salt and use a rubber spatula to stir until just combined and no dry flour remains.

4. Use a large spoon and the rubber spatula to distribute the batter evenly among the 12 greased cupcake liners. Place one caramel in the centre of each portion of batter. Sprinkle each portion with the flaky salt, dividing it evenly.

5. Place the muffin tin in the oven. Bake until a toothpick inserted into one brownie edge (not the caramel centre!) comes out with a few crumbs attached (see page 12), 32 to 36 minutes.

!! 6. Use oven mitts to remove the muffin tin from the oven and place it on the hob or a cooling rack. Let the brownie bites cool in the muffin tin for 20 to 30 minutes. Serve warm or at room temperature.

SALTED CHOCOLATE-FILLED BROWNIE BITES

Use 12 chocolates instead of caramels, pressing them down into the brownie batter.

 **FUN FOOD FACT**

During the colonial period in India, England imposed a tax on salt. Famed civil rights activist Mahatma Gandhi organized a march to the sea to collect salt. He did not want women to participate. But freedom fighter Kamaladevi Chattopadhyay disagreed and organized women to collect and sell salt in defiance of the British rules. She mobilized countless women to be on the frontlines of the salt protests, and together they helped bring an end to colonial rule.

MEET CHEF JOANNE CHANG

If you had told young Joanne that she would grow up to be a pastry chef, she wouldn't have believed you. Raised by immigrant parents in a traditional Taiwanese household, she rarely had sweets. Her family ate orange slices for dessert most days. On special occasions, her mum might slice up a mango.

Joanne studied mathematics and economics at Harvard University. So how did she end up as an award-winning baker and cookbook author? She started baking at home and throwing dinner parties for friends. Her colleagues at the consulting firm where she worked got to enjoy *a lot* of her homemade cookies.

After a few years, Joanne made the leap. She took jobs in restaurants and bakeries in Boston and New York and zeroed in on her true passion: pastries. She learned from American, French, and Mediterranean chefs and explored techniques from the Taiwanese dishes she grew up with to come up with her own cooking style. She describes it as "simple and classic favourites made with the freshest, highest-quality ingredients". When she develops a new recipe, she puts it to a simple test by asking one question: does it taste so good that you just want to keep eating it? If the answer is yes, she knows the recipe is a keeper.

In 2000, she opened Flour Bakery in Boston, USA. Now, there are nine locations. Joanne is also the author of five cookbooks.

One dessert that has a special place in Joanne's heart is shaved ice with sweetened condensed milk and mangoes. It's her mum's favourite dessert, and Joanne eats it every day when she visits Taiwan.

HOMEMADE OREOS

MAKES 16 TO 18 SANDWICH COOKIES

"Homemade Oreos are quite a big project for one day! If you'd like to split it up, prepare the dough through step 3, wrap it in cling film, and store it in the fridge for up to 1 week or in the freezer for up to 1 month. If freezing, move the dough to the fridge to thaw the day before you want to bake the cookies." —Joanne Chang

!!1. **For the cookies:** Put the chocolate chips into a small microwave-safe bowl. Heat in a microwave at 50 per cent power for 3 to 5 minutes, stopping every minute and stirring with a silicone spatula, until melted and smooth. Use oven gloves to remove the bowl from the microwave and place it on the worktop.

2. In a large bowl, whisk together the melted butter and granulated sugar until well mixed. Whisk in the vanilla and the melted chocolate until blended. Then whisk in the egg, mixing well.

3. In a medium bowl, use a wooden spoon to stir together the flour, cocoa powder, bicarbonate of soda, and salt until well mixed. Stir the flour mixture into the chocolate mixture. The dough will start to seem too floury. At this point, use your hands to mix and knead the dough until it comes together and no dry flour remains, about 1 minute. It will be ready when it has the consistency of Play-Doh.

4. Cover the bowl with cling film and let the dough sit for about 1 hour at room temperature to firm up.

5. Lay a 38 cm (15 in) square sheet of parchment paper on a worktop. Turn the dough out onto the parchment paper. Use your hands to shape the dough into a rough log about 25 cm (10 in) long and 6 cm (2½ in) wide. Place the log at the edge of the parchment sheet and roll the parchment around the log. With the log fully encased in the parchment, use your hands to roll it into a smoother log (still 6 cm (2½ in) wide). Twist the ends of the parchment paper closed to fully encase the log. Wrap the parchment-wrapped log in cling film and chill in the fridge until firm, at least 2 hours. The dough log may settle and sink a bit in the fridge. If you'd like to keep a nice round log shape, reroll it every 15 minutes or so to help it keep its shape.

6. Set an oven rack in the middle position and heat the oven to 170°C. Line two baking trays with parchment paper.

INGREDIENTS

Cookies

170 g dark chocolate chips, melted

240 g unsalted butter, melted and cooled (see page 11)

165 g granulated sugar

1 teaspoon vanilla extract

1 egg

190 g plain flour

75 g unsweetened Dutch-processed cocoa powder

½ teaspoon bicarbonate of soda

1 teaspoon kosher salt

Filling

120 g unsalted butter, softened (see page 11)

1 teaspoon vanilla extract

200 g icing sugar

1 tablespoon milk

Pinch of table salt

COOKIES, BROWNIES, AND BARS

If Joanne could host any woman at an awesome dinner party, she'd invite Michelle Obama and Dorie Greenspan. She would make classic Taiwanese dishes from her childhood: mapo tofu, pea pod stems with garlic, chicken braised with star anise and ginger, and lots of white rice.

HOMEMADE OREOS
CONTINUED

> Joanne's favourite person to cook with is her husband. "We have so much fun together," she says. "He is very meticulous, I tend to be more free-form, and we meet in the middle."

7 Take the dough log out of the fridge and place on a **chopping board**. Remove the cling film and parchment. Use a **bench scraper** or **chef's knife** to cut the log into slices about 5 cm (¼ in) thick. Place the slices about 2.5 cm (1 in) apart on the parchment-lined baking trays, arranging half of the slices on each baking tray.

!! 8 Place one baking tray in the oven. Bake until the cookies are firm to the touch, 18 to 22 minutes. Ask a grown-up to help you test if they are firm or not. As soon as they feel firm, you'll need to remove them from the oven. You can't judge by colour because they start out looking black!

!! 9 While the cookies are baking, make the cream filling: In a **stand mixer** fitted with the **paddle attachment** or in a **large bowl** if using a **handheld mixer**, beat the softened butter on low speed until smooth, about 30 seconds. Stop the mixer.

10 Add the vanilla and icing sugar and beat on low speed until a smooth paste forms, about 2 minutes.

11 Stop the mixer and use a **rubber spatula** to scrape down the sides of the bowl and the paddle or beaters. Add the milk and salt and beat on low speed until well combined and very smooth, about 2 minutes. It will look like very thick frosting and feel like putty. The filling will keep in an **airtight container** at room temperature for up to 2 days or in the fridge for up to 2 weeks. Bring to room temperature before using.

12 Use **oven gloves** to remove the baking tray from the oven and place it on the hob or a **cooling rack**. Repeat step 8 to bake the second batch of cookies. Let the cookies cool to room temperature on the baking trays, about 30 minutes.

13 Use a **tablespoon** to scoop out a level spoonful of the vanilla cream filling and place it on one cookie. Use a **butter knife** or **offset spatula** to spread out the filling, leaving some room around the edges. Place a second cookie on top, gently press the cookies together, and serve. The cookies can be stored in an airtight container at room temperature for up to 3 days.

MAKES 9 SQUARES

CEREAL TREATS YOUR WAY

INGREDIENTS

Vegetable oil spray

90 g unsalted butter

275 g bag mini marshmallows

50 g crispy rice cereal

50 g fruit puff cereal or peanut butter puff cereal

50 g multigrain hoop cereal

Choose your own cereal treat adventure! This recipe uses three kinds of cereal, but you can use any cereals you want. Try different combinations or use 150 g of one cereal. We know it's hard to wait, but it's important for the cereal treats to cool completely before cutting, or they won't hold their shape. Even if they feel cool on the outside, they might still be warm in the middle.

1. Spray the inside of an **20 cm (8 in) square metal baking tin** with vegetable oil spray.

2. In a **casserole dish** or **other large, heavy pot**, melt the butter on the hob over medium heat.

3. Add the marshmallows to the pot and cook, stirring constantly with a **silicone spatula**, until the marshmallows are fully melted, about 3 minutes. Turn off the hob and slide the pot to a cool part of the hob.

4. Working quickly, gently stir in all of the cereal until completely coated in the marshmallow mixture.

!!5. Transfer the cereal mixture to the prepared baking tin.

6. Rinse the spatula but do not dry it. Use the wet spatula to press and smooth the cereal mixture into an even layer.

7. Let the cereal treats cool at room temperature for at least 1 hour.

!!8. Run a **butter knife** along the edges of the tin to release the treats. Turn the slab of treats out onto a **chopping board**. Use a **chef's knife** to cut the slab into thirds in one direction. Then cut the slab into thirds in the other direction. You'll end up with nine squares. Serve.

REBEL IN THE KITCHEN

In the 1930s, Mildred Day and Malitta Jensen worked for Kellogg's, the maker of Rice Krispies. They developed the original recipe for a cereal treat made with Rice Krispies. It has been printed on cereal boxes since 1941, though the company has updated the recipe a few times over the years. The original recipe called for treacle instead of marshmallows.

MAKES 16 SQUARES

BROOKIES

INGREDIENTS

Brownie Batter
Vegetable oil spray

45 g unsalted butter, melted and cooled (see page 11)

75 ml vegetable oil

1 large egg

165 g granulated sugar

60 g plain flour

25 g unsweetened Dutch-processed cocoa powder

¼ teaspoon table salt

Cookie Batter
95 g light brown sugar

60 g unsalted butter, melted and cooled (see page 11)

1 large egg

½ teaspoon vanilla extract

60 g plain flour

¼ teaspoon baking powder

45 g dark chocolate chips

Brookies are perfect when you don't know if you want brownies or cookies. Half brownie, half chocolate chip cookie, these bars are ideal for the indecisive. Plus, two batters mean double the spatulas to lick!

1. Set an oven rack in the middle position and heat the oven to 170°C. Make an **aluminium foil** sling for an **20 cm (8 in) square metal baking tin** (see page 13). Spray the foil lightly and evenly with vegetable oil spray.

2. For the brownie batter: in a **medium bowl**, **whisk** together the 45 g melted butter, the oil, and 1 egg until blended. Add the granulated sugar, 60 g flour, cocoa powder, and salt and whisk until well combined and no dry ingredients remain. Set aside.

3. For the cookie batter: in a second **medium bowl**, whisk together the brown sugar, 60 g melted butter, 1 egg, and vanilla until blended. Add the 60 g flour and baking powder and use a **rubber spatula** to stir until no dry flour remains. Add the chocolate chips and stir to distribute evenly.

4. Use a **large spoon** to drop scoops of each batter into the foil-lined baking tin. Don't worry about where they wind up. The scoops can be random and overlap one another. Once all of both batters are in the tin, use the spatula to smooth the mixed batters into an even layer.

5. Place the baking tin in the oven. Bake until a toothpick inserted into the centre comes out with a few crumbs attached (see page 12), 30 to 35 minutes.

⚠ 6. Use **oven gloves** to remove the baking tin from the oven and place it on the hob or a **cooling rack**. Let the brookies cool completely in the tin, about 1 hour.

7. Holding the edges of the foil sling, carefully lift the bars out of the baking tin and onto a **chopping board**. Use a **chef's knife** to cut the slab of bars into fourths in one direction, then cut the slab into fourths in the other direction. You'll end up with 16 squares. Serve.

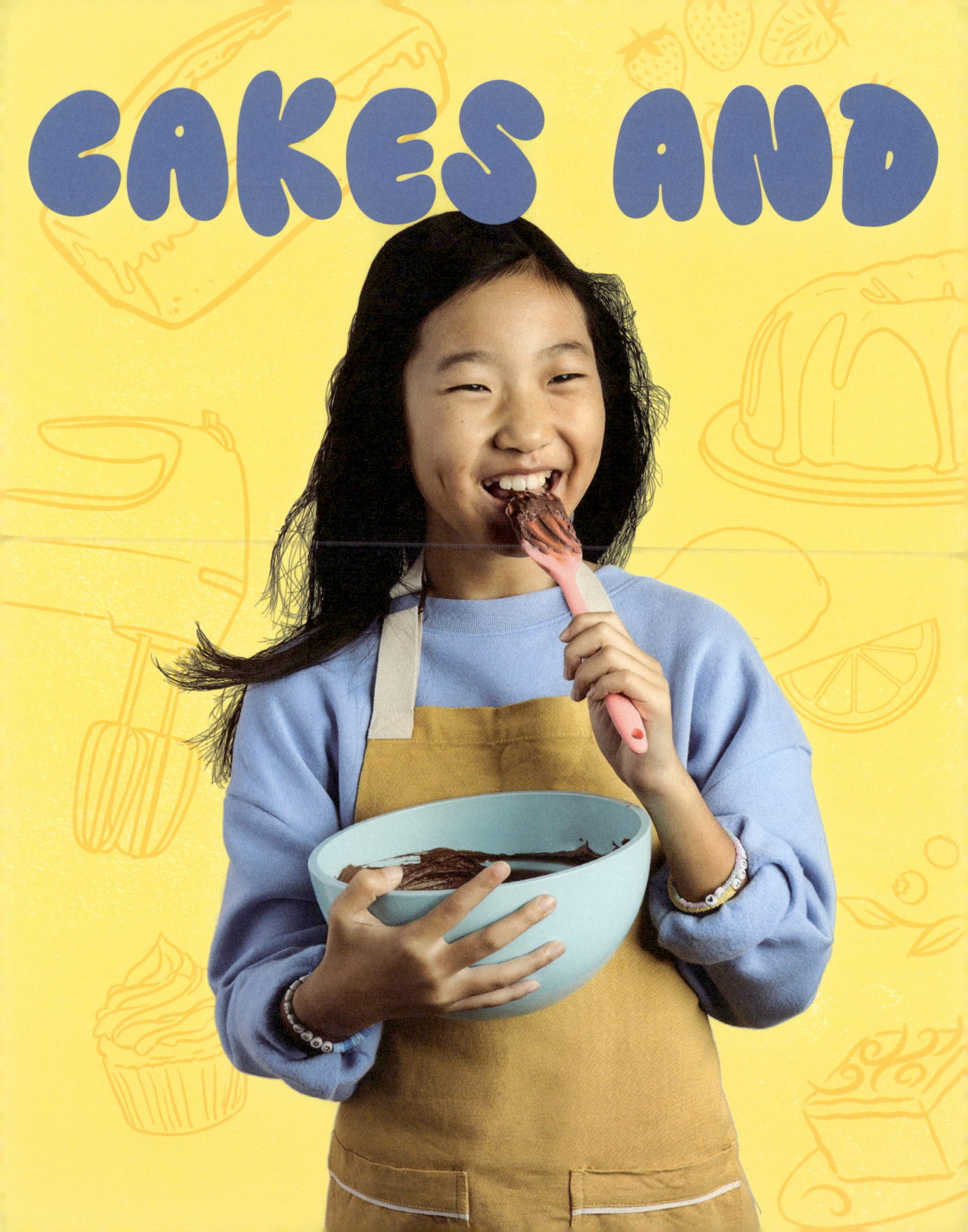

CUPCAKES

71	Confetti Sheet Cake
72	Red Velvet Cupcakes
74	Cream Cheese Icing
75	Vanilla Buttercream Confetti Buttercream
77	Basic Cake (in a Blender) by Chef Jennifer Latham
80	Bolo de Cenoura
83	Victoria Sponge
89	One-Bowl Courgette Spice Cake by Chef Vallery Lomas
90	Chocolate–Peanut Butter Mug Cake
92	Lemon Pound Cake Lemon–Poppy Seed Pound Cake
95	Strawberry Snacking Cake by Chef Rachel Gurjar
98	Orange Semolina Cake
101	Pear and Cardamom Loaf Cake by Chef Nadiya Hussain
104	Flourless Chocolate Cake
109	Chocolate Chip Mochi Muffins by Chef Alana Kysar
110	Tres Leches de Coco Pastel de Tres Leches
114	Coffee Crumb Cake
117	No-Bake Cheesecake with Any-Cookie Crust

Confetti Sheet Cake

SERVES 12 TO 15

Round, sequin-like sprinkles make this cake look like birthday-party confetti, but sprinkles in any shape or size will give it a festive and colourful look. There are no eggs or butter in this recipe, so if you want to make it vegan, use plant-based milk. Cake flour produces an extra soft, tender, and fluffy crumb, but if plain is what you have on hand, you can use it instead. The cake will be a bit denser but still delicious. For double the rainbow sprinkle power, top with Confetti Buttercream (page 75). If you're making your cake vegan, use just icing sugar or a shop-bought vegan icing as the topping.

INGREDIENTS

Vegetable oil spray

380 g plain flour or cake flour

330 g granulated sugar

1 tablespoon baking powder

1 teaspoon table salt

500 ml milk or plant-based milk of choice

120 ml vegetable oil

2 tablespoons fresh lemon juice (see page 12)

1 tablespoon vanilla extract

95 g rainbow sprinkles

Icing sugar, for dusting, or 1 recipe Confetti Buttercream (page 75)

1. Set an oven rack in the middle position and heat the oven to 180°C. Spray the inside of a **23 by 33 cm (9 by 13 in) metal baking tin** with vegetable oil spray.

2. In a **large bowl**, **whisk** together the flour, granulated sugar, baking powder, and salt. Add the milk, vegetable oil, lemon juice, and vanilla and whisk until the batter is well mixed and smooth.

3. Add the sprinkles to the batter and use a **rubber spatula** to stir gently until evenly distributed. Use the spatula to scrape the batter into the greased baking tin.

4. Place the baking tin in the oven. Bake until the top of the cake is light golden brown and a **toothpick** inserted into the centre of the cake comes out clean (see page 12), 35 to 40 minutes.

!! 5. Use **oven gloves** to remove the baking tin from the oven and place it on the hob or a **cooling rack**. Let the cake cool completely in the tin, at least 2 hours.

6. Use a **butter knife** to loosen the edges of the cake from the tin. If using icing sugar, use a **fine-mesh sieve** to sprinkle the top of the cake with the sugar (see page 16). If using the buttercream, use an **offset spatula** or the butter knife to spread it in an even layer over the top of the cake. Cut the cake into pieces and serve.

 FUN FOOD FACT

Swedish YouTuber Therése Lindgren set a Guinness World Record for baking the largest vegan cake. Made with semolina, soy yoghurt, strawberries, and other ingredients, it weighed more than 454 kg (1,000 pounds)!

CAKES AND CUPCAKES

MAKES 12 CUPCAKES

RED VELVET CUPCAKES

INGREDIENTS

Vegetable oil spray

155 g plain flour

2 tablespoons unsweetened natural cocoa powder

½ teaspoon baking powder

½ teaspoon bicarbonate of soda

½ teaspoon table salt

200 g granulated sugar

75 ml buttermilk

120 ml vegetable oil

1 large egg

1 tablespoon red liquid food colouring

1 teaspoon vanilla extract

½ teaspoon distilled white vinegar

1 recipe Cream Cheese Icing (page 74)

Unsweetened natural cocoa powder works best in this recipe. It's more acidic than Dutch-processed cocoa powder and, along with the acidic buttermilk and vinegar in the batter, it will react with the bicarbonate of soda to produce a light and fluffy cake. That chemical reaction also helps to turn the batter red! A traditional red velvet cake uses only cocoa for colouring, but for extra vibrancy, this recipe calls for red food colouring as well. Cream Cheese Icing (page 74) is a classic topping for red velvet cakes and cupcakes, but Vanilla Buttercream (page 75), Confetti Buttercream (page 75), or a shop-bought icing of your choice can be used instead.

1. Set an oven rack in the middle position and heat the oven to 170°C. Line a **12-hole muffin tin** with **cupcake liners**. Spray the top of the muffin tin with vegetable oil spray (this helps keep the edges of the cupcakes from sticking to the tin).

2. In a **medium bowl**, **whisk** together the flour, cocoa powder, baking powder, bicarbonate of soda, and salt.

3. In a **large bowl**, whisk together the sugar, buttermilk, oil, egg, food colouring, vanilla, and vinegar until well combined.

4. Add the flour mixture to the sugar mixture and whisk until no dry flour remains and the mixture is smooth.

5. Divide the batter evenly among the cupcake liners. Use a **spoon** or **small rubber spatula** to help scrape the batter into the liners.

6. Place the muffin tin in the oven. Bake until the cupcakes are rounded and shiny on top and a **toothpick** inserted into the centre of a cupcake comes out clean (see page 12), 25 to 30 minutes.

!! 7. Use **oven gloves** to remove the muffin tin from the oven and place it on the hob or a **cooling rack**. Let the cupcakes cool in the tin for 15 to 20 minutes.

8. Use your fingertips to carefully wiggle each cupcake loose from the tin and transfer them directly to a cooling rack. Let the cupcakes cool completely before icing, at least 30 minutes. Add the icing and serve.

👨‍🍳 REBEL IN THE KITCHEN

The colour in early red velvet cakes came from cocoa powder. Later on, people began using food colouring. During World War II, sugar and butter were rationed. Some cooks used beetroot or beetroot juice to ensure their cakes were moist and flavourful – and red. Keeping that tradition alive, Pamela Moxley, a pastry chef in Atlanta, USA, recently developed a red velvet cake recipe that calls for beetroot. She uses cocoa powder and lemon juice along with the beetroot to make the cake a bright, rich red.

CREAM CHEESE ICING

MAKES AROUND 750 G ICING

INGREDIENTS

340 g full-fat cream cheese, cut into 2.5 cm (1 in) pieces and softened (see page 11)

120 g unsalted butter, cut into 8 equal pieces and softened (see page 11)

290 g icing sugar

1 teaspoon vanilla extract

Big pinch of table salt

1 tablespoon sour cream (optional)

Use this light and luscious icing to add a nice layer of tanginess to sweet treats. A dollop of sour cream gives the icing a boost of tartness, but you can skip it if you like your icing on the sweeter side. For extra-smooth icing, make sure your cream cheese and butter are well softened before starting.

1. Add the softened cream cheese and softened butter to the bowl of a **stand mixer** fitted with the **paddle attachment** or to a **large bowl** if you're using a **handheld mixer**. Beat the mixture on high speed until very smooth and airy, about 2 minutes. Stop the mixer.

2. Use a **rubber spatula** to scrape down the sides of the bowl and the paddle or beaters. Start the mixer on low speed and slowly add the icing sugar, adding in a little at a time. Continue to beat the mixture until all of the sugar has been incorporated, 1 to 2 minutes. Stop the mixer.

3. Scrape down the sides of the bowl. Add the vanilla, salt, and sour cream (if using). Beat on high speed until the icing is light and fluffy, about 2 minutes. Stop the mixer.

4. Remove the paddle or beaters and scrape any icing sticking to them into the bowl. Gently stir the icing one more time. Time to ice your cupcakes or cake!

FUN FOOD FACT

Many cakes are covered with frosting or icing. One of the earliest sweet cake toppers was described by Rebecca Price in *The Compleat Cook* in 1655. To finish her almond cakes, she instructed home cooks to "mingle" sugar with rose water until it is as thick as pudding, then use a feather to ice the sides of the cake.

Vanilla Buttercream

MAKES AROUND 750 G ICING

Use liquid or gel food colouring to create buttercream and icings in any colour you like! The trick with food colouring is to add a little bit at a time. Otherwise, the colour might come out darker than you want. You can also swap the vanilla extract for a different flavour extract, such as peppermint, coconut, orange, or raspberry. If trying one of these flavours, use only ½ teaspoon extract, as they all impart a much stronger flavour than vanilla.

1. Add the softened butter to the bowl of a **stand mixer** fitted with the **paddle attachment** or to a **large bowl** if you're using a **handheld mixer**. Start the mixer on low speed and slowly add the icing sugar, adding a little at a time. Continue to beat the mixture until all of the sugar has been incorporated, 1 to 2 minutes. Stop the mixer.

2. Use a **rubber spatula** to scrape down the sides of the bowl and the paddle or beaters. Add the vanilla and salt. Beat on medium speed until the buttercream is light and fluffy, about 5 minutes, stopping the mixer and scraping down the sides of the bowl and the paddle or beaters with the rubber spatula a couple of times along the way. Stop the mixer.

3. Scrape down the sides of the bowl. Add the cream and food colouring (if using). Beat on low speed until the cream is fully incorporated, 30 seconds to 1 minute. Increase the speed to medium and beat until the buttercream is fluffy, about 30 seconds. Stop the mixer.

4. Remove the paddle or beaters and scrape any buttercream sticking to them into the bowl. Gently stir the it once more. Time to ice your cake or cupcakes!

Confetti Buttercream

Stir in 60 g rainbow sprinkles at the end of step 4.

Ingredients

300 g unsalted butter, cut into 1-tablespoon pieces and softened (see page 11)

290 g icing sugar

2 teaspoons vanilla extract

¼ teaspoon table salt

75 ml double cream

Liquid or gel food colouring in colour of choice (optional)

Fun Food Fact

After meeting with vanilla growers in Mexico in 1994, Patricia Rain decided it was her "destiny to support and promote not only pure vanilla but also those who grow it". Women produce up to 80 per cent of the vanilla grown in developing countries but receive very little money for their work. Known as the Vanilla Queen, Patricia launched The Vanilla Company in 2001. She advocates for vanilla farmers – especially women – to receive fair wages.

MEET CHEF JENNIFER LATHAM

For Jennifer, cooking is a family tradition. She remembers making chocolate mousse pie with her mum when she was a kid. She held her breath as her mum turned the bowl of whipped egg whites upside down over her head. And then she laughed with relief when she saw the whites were stiff enough. They held their shape and didn't spill onto her head.

Now, as a grown-up, she loves to cook with her kids. Together, they learn and laugh and have great fun in the kitchen. And that chocolate mousse pie is still a favourite. Jennifer's mother got the recipe from a 1980 issue of *Bon Appétit* magazine, and Jennifer whips it up at least once a year. "It's not my birthday without that pie," she says.

Jennifer describes her recipes as California style, with lots of fresh ingredients and simple presentations. She says, "I love the building-block recipes, like a perfect flaky crust or an ice cream base that you can dress up and use a million different ways." Plus, she's an expert baker! Sourdough loaves, dinner rolls, focaccia pizza, monkey bread – she makes them all. The author of *Baking Bread with Kids*, she also wrote *Bread Book* with Chad Robertson.

Her advice to budding chefs? It doesn't have to be super fancy to be good. Sometimes the simplest foods are the most satisfying.

If Jennifer could invite any famous woman from the past or present to dinner, she would choose science fiction author Ursula K. Le Guin. "I never get over her combination of vivid imagination, uncanny prescience, and knife-sharp social criticism," she says. "I'd probably make cioppino because I love one-pot brothy meals – especially seafood ones – that go with crusty sourdough bread."

Basic Cake (in a Blender)

MAKES ONE 23 CM (9 IN) CAKE, ONE 26 CM (10 IN) BUNDT CAKE, OR TWO 15 CM (6 IN) CAKES

"This cake is softer and more moist than most yellow cakes, thanks to lots of eggs and butter (which also makes it delicious). A pro tip I learned at my first-ever baking job is to sift the flour and baking powder together three times instead of just once. It helps distribute the baking powder throughout the batter and will give you an extra fluffy cake. When making the icing, make sure the butter is very soft to ensure a smooth and quick mixing process." —Jennifer Latham

1. For the cake: Set an oven rack in the middle position and heat the oven to 170°C. Line the bottom of a 23 cm (9 in) round cake tin or two 15 cm (6 in) cake tins with parchment paper (see page 14). If using a 26 cm (10 in) bundt tin, skip the parchment paper step.

2. Use a pastry brush to lightly brush the inside walls of your cake tin(s) with the melted butter (this little bit won't take away enough from the cake to make a difference). Use a large fine-mesh sieve to dust the sides lightly with flour, until all sides are coated. Set aside.

3. Using the large fine-mesh sieve, sift together the flour and baking powder into a large bowl, tapping the side of the sieve until all of the flour mixture goes through. Set aside.

4. Add the 250 ml milk, the sugar, oil, and the rest of the melted butter to a blender. Put the lid on and pulse a few times until just combined. Add the eggs and blend on medium-high speed until the mixture is lighter in colour and very smooth, about 1 minute.

5. Remove the lid and add the ½ teaspoon salt and 2 teaspoons vanilla. Put the lid back on and pulse a few times to combine.

6. Pour the contents of the blender jug into the bowl with the flour mixture. Using a rubber spatula, stir gently until combined and most of the lumps are smoothed out (a few tiny lumps are OK).

7. Pour the batter into the prepared tin(s). (If using two 15 cm (6 in) pans, divide it evenly between the tins.) Tap the tin(s) gently on the worktop twice to make sure there are no large air bubbles.

INGREDIENTS

Cake

120 g unsalted butter, melted and cooled (see page 11)

280 g plain flour, plus more for dusting

2 teaspoons baking powder

250 ml whole milk

330 g granulated sugar

120 ml sunflower oil or other neutral oil

4 large eggs, at room temperature

½ teaspoon fine sea salt

2 teaspoons vanilla extract

Chocolate Icing

75 g unsweetened natural or Dutch-processed cocoa powder (Dutch-processed powder will give more of milk-chocolatey flavour)

500 g icing sugar

continued

CONTINUED

Basic Cake (in a Blender)
continued

8. Place the tin(s) in the oven. Bake until the top is golden brown and a *toothpick* inserted into the centre comes out clean (see page 12), about 1 hour for 15 cm (6 in) cake tins and 1 hour and 5 minutes to 1 hour and 10 minutes for a 23 cm (9 in) cake tin or a 26 cm (10 in) Bundt tin.

9. **While the cake is baking, make the chocolate icing:** Using a *large fine-mesh sieve*, sift together the cocoa powder and icing sugar into a *large bowl*. Set aside.

10. Add the 180 g softened butter, ½ teaspoon vanilla, and 1 teaspoon salt to the bowl of a *stand mixer* fitted with the *paddle attachment* or to a *large bowl* if using a *handheld mixer*. Beat on low speed until combined, about 1 minute. Stop the mixer.

11. Use a *rubber spatula* to scrape down the sides of the bowl. Add 1 mugful of the cocoa-sugar mixture and beat on low speed until incorporated, about 1 minute. Add 3 tablespoons of the milk and beat on low speed until incorporated, about 30 seconds. Repeat, alternating additions of the cocoa-sugar mixture and milk, until all the cocoa mixture and milk are added and combined. Stop the mixer. Use the rubber spatula to scrape down the sides and along the bottom of the bowl. If the frosting seems stiff, add another tablespoon of milk at a time and mix on medium speed until combined. Set aside.

!!12. Use *oven gloves* to remove the tin(s) from the oven and place on the hob or a *cooling rack*. Let the cake(s) cool completely in the tin(s), about 2 hours.

!!13. Turn the cake(s) out of the tin(s) (see page 15). Place one cake or the Bundt cake on a *serving plate.* If you made a 23 cm (9 in) cake, use a *serrated knife* to carefully cut the cake round in half horizontally (through the middle). Put the bottom half, bottom side down, on a serving plate.

14. **To decorate:** Spread about half of the icing over the top of the bottom layer or first cake. Place the top layer or second cake, cut side down, on top and spread the rest of the icing on top. You can also spread the icing over the sides. Decorate with whatever sprinkles, sparklers, and/or bonbons you fancy.

---

180 g unsalted butter, softened (see page 11)

½ teaspoon vanilla extract

1 teaspoon fine sea salt

120 ml whole milk, plus 1 to 2 tablespoons more as needed

Sprinkles, bonbons, and/or edible glitter, for decorating (optional)

BOLO DE CENOURA

SERVES 12 TO 14

INGREDIENTS

Cake
Vegetable oil spray
220 g plain flour
2 teaspoons baking powder
1 teaspoon table salt
3 medium carrots, scrubbed, trimmed, and cut into 1 cm (½ in) thick slices
365 g granulated sugar
175 ml vegetable oil
3 large eggs

Chocolate Glaze
90 g dark chocolate chips
45 g unsalted butter, cut into 1-tablespoon pieces
Pinch of table salt

If you've ever grated carrots for a traditional American carrot cake, you know it's a labour of love (and occasionally the cause of some grazed knuckles!). This Brazilian carrot cake skips the grating and blends the carrots instead. You don't even need to peel them first. The powerful motor of a food processor makes it a snap to puree the carrots into a smooth mixture for the cake batter. If you have a heavy-duty blender, you can use that instead. Just make sure that no chunks of carrot block the blades from spinning. The blended carrots make this cake a beautiful bright orange and super fluffy. It is extra pretty baked in a Bundt tin, but if you don't have one, you can use a 23 cm (9 in) round cake tin instead.

1. **For the cake:** Set an oven rack in the middle position and heat the oven to 180°C. Spray the inside of a **26 cm (10 in) Bundt tin** very well with vegetable oil spray.

2. In a **large bowl, whisk** together the flour, baking powder, and salt.

3. Add the carrots, sugar, oil, and eggs to a **food processor**. Place the lid on the food processor and lock it into place. Process until the carrots break down and the mixture is totally smooth, about 1 minute. Stop the processor.

!! 4. Remove the processor lid and carefully remove the processor blade. Use a **rubber spatula** to transfer the carrot mixture to the large bowl with the flour mixture.

5. Stir gently with the spatula until no dry flour remains (make sure to scrape along the bottom and sides of the bowl). Scrape the batter into the greased Bundt tin.

6. Place the Bundt tin in the oven. Bake until the cake is golden brown and a **toothpick** inserted into the centre comes out clean (see page 12), 40 to 45 minutes.

!! 7. Use **oven gloves** to remove the Bundt tin from the oven and place it on the hob or a **cooling rack**. Let the cake cool in the tin for 15 minutes.

CONTINUED

BOLO DE CENOURA
CONTINUED

!! 8 Place another **cooling rack**, top side down, on top of the Bundt tin. Use oven gloves to hold the tin against the rack, flip the tin and rack over together, and set the rack on the worktop. Lift the Bundt tin off the cake and set the tin on the hob to cool. Let the cake cool completely on the rack, about 1½ hours.

9 **For the glaze:** When the cake is cool, set the cooling rack with the cake on it in a **baking tray**. In a **medium microwave-safe bowl**, combine the chocolate chips, butter, and pinch of salt. Microwave at 50 per cent power until melted, 2 to 3 minutes. Stop the microwave every 30 seconds and stir the mixture with a **spoon** to see if it has melted.

10 Remove the bowl from the microwave and stir the mixture until completely melted and smooth. Spoon the glaze around the top of the cake, letting it drip down the sides. Let sit for at least 15 minutes to allow the glaze to set. Cut into slices and serve.

YOU'RE THE CHEF!
"It's an amazing dish with incredible flavour and texture. The carrot and chocolate go well together. Blending the carrots really makes the cake absolutely stunning!"
—Althea, 10

REBEL GIRLS MAKE DESSERT

VICTORIA SPONGE

SERVES 8 TO 10

A Victoria sponge (also called a Vicky sponge or a Victoria sandwich) is a simple British cake enjoyed at teatime. It's named for Queen Victoria, who is said to have eaten a slice of it every afternoon. Make sure that your butter is well softened so it becomes nice and creamy when you beat it with the mixer. This cake gets part of its lift from the air whipped into the butter and sugar.

INGREDIENTS

Vegetable oil spray

190 g plain flour

1 tablespoon baking powder

½ teaspoon table salt

210 g unsalted butter, softened (see page 11)

200 g granulated sugar

4 large eggs, cracked into a small bowl

75 ml milk

1 recipe Whipped Cream (page 17)

160 g raspberry jam

Icing sugar, for dusting

1. Set an oven rack in the middle position and heat the oven to 180°C. Spray the inside of **two 20 cm (8 in) round cake tins** with vegetable oil spray. Line each cake tin with a circle of **parchment paper** (see page 14).

2. In a **medium bowl**, **whisk** together the flour, baking powder, and salt.

3. Add the softened butter and granulated sugar to the bowl of a **stand mixer** fitted with the **paddle attachment** or to a **large bowl** if you're using a **handheld mixer**. Beat on medium speed until the ingredients are creamy and fluffy, about 3 minutes. Stop the mixer.

4. Use a **rubber spatula** to scrape down the sides of the bowl. With the mixer running on low speed, add the eggs one at a time, beating after each addition until incorporated, about 30 seconds. (To add them one at a time, carefully tip the bowl with the eggs towards the bowl with the butter-sugar mixture until a yolk plops out. It will take its egg white with it. Repeat until all the yolks and whites are added.) Stop the mixer.

5. Scrape down the sides of the bowl with the spatula. Add the milk and half of the flour mixture. Beat on low speed until combined, about 30 seconds. Stop the mixer, add the remaining flour mixture, and then beat on low speed until fully combined, about 30 more seconds. Stop the mixer. Remove the paddle or beaters and use the spatula to scrape any batter sticking to them into the bowl.

6. To make sure no dry flour remains, use the spatula to give the batter a good stir, scraping along the bottom and sides of the bowl. Divide the batter evenly between the two greased parchment-lined cake tins. Use the spatula to spread the batter into an even layer in each tin and smooth the top.

CONTINUED

CAKES AND CUPCAKES

VICTORIA SPONGE
CONTINUED

7 Place the cake tins in the oven. Bake until the cake layers are puffy and light golden brown on top and a **toothpick** inserted into the centre of each layer comes out clean (see page 12), 24 to 28 minutes.

!!8 Use **oven gloves** to remove the cake tins from the oven and place them on the hob or a **cooling rack**. Let the cakes cool in the tins for 15 minutes.

!!9 Using oven gloves, one at a time, turn the cakes out of their tins (see page 15). Let the cakes cool completely on the rack, at least 1 hour.

10 When you're ready to assemble your cake, whip the cream to stiff peaks (see page 17).

11 Transfer one cooled cake round (the one you think is the least pretty of the two), bottom side down, to a **serving plate**. Use an **offset spatula** or a **butter knife** to spread the top of the cake evenly with the jam. Rinse and dry the offset spatula or butter knife.

12 Dollop half of the whipped cream over the jam. Use the offset spatula or butter knife to spread it into an even layer, stopping about 1 cm (½ in) from the edge of the cake.

13 Place the second cake round, bottom side down, on top of the whipped cream and press down gently to stick the layers together (the cream will push out closer to the edges but shouldn't squish out of the sides).

14 Use a **fine-mesh sieve** to sprinkle the top of the cake with icing sugar (see page 16).

!!15 Use a **serrated knife** to carefully saw the cake into wedges (some cream and jam may squish out of the sides, but that's OK!). Serve with the remaining whipped cream on the side.

YOU'RE THE CHEF!
"The cake tasted rich and the raspberry jam added a bright burst of flavour. My favourite part was the homemade whipped cream, which was creamy and sweet!"
—Savannah, 11

If Vallery could give advice to her young self, she'd remind herself to enjoy the process and to have fun and experiment more.

Fresh fruits and vegetables have been part of Vallery's life since she was little. In the spring, she would run up and down the garden rows, plucking the plump, juicy strawberries that grew on her father's property. The berries seemed endless, and so was the joy they brought her.

When she thinks back to her earliest kitchen memories, she sees her mother standing by the oven stirring a large pot of homemade jam. She also pictures her dad with a wok, tossing vegetables as he makes his signature dish, stir-fry.

Vallery grew up, went off to college, and enrolled in law school. Through all of the reading, studying, and exams, she never lost her love for food and cooking. After eight years practicing law, she decided to make a change. She quit her job, found an apartment with a bigger kitchen, and dedicated herself to developing her recipes.

Vallery loves baking with fresh, in-season fruits and other ingredients native to her home state of Louisiana, USA, like pecans and strawberries. She says her style is "comforting, approachable, and flavourful, with classics like cream cheese pound cake and bourbon pecan pie."

In 2017, Vallery won *The Great American Baking Show*. She hosts the online US cooking show *Vallery Bakes Your Questions*, and her book, *Life Is What You Bake It*, is packed with delightful recipes, like cornmeal pancakes, chocolate mint moon pies, and her granny's million dollar cake.

The guest list for Vallery's dream dinner party would include iconic chefs Edna Lewis and Leah Chase and her grandmother Leona Clay Johnson. "These women have all inspired me and been culinary beacons," says Vallery. "It would truly be special to see them all converse together."

CAKES AND CUPCAKES

One-Bowl Courgette Spice Cake

SERVES 8 TO 10

"Everyone needs a moist, flavourful cake like this one in their repertoire. For this recipe, you can use shop-bought buttermilk or make your own by adding 1 teaspoon lemon juice or distilled white vinegar to 60 ml milk. The milk will start to curdle after 5 minutes, which is what you're looking for. For the courgette, grate it on the large holes of a grater. Make sure to squeeze the grated courgette over the sink to release its liquid, leaving only a little liquid behind. You can store the cake in a cake dome or airtight container in the fridge for up to 1 week." —Vallery Lomas

1. **For the cake:** Set an oven rack in the middle position and heat the oven to 180°C. Spray the inside of a 23 cm (9 in) round cake tin with vegetable oil spray.

2. In a large bowl, whisk together the eggs, oil, buttermilk, granulated sugar, and ¼ teaspoon salt until well mixed. It will resemble a yellowish mayonnaise.

3. Add the flour, bicarbonate of soda, baking powder, cinnamon, and ginger. Whisk well to combine. The batter will resemble a loose muffin batter.

4. Add the courgette and pecans. Use a rubber spatula to stir until evenly incorporated. Scrape the batter into the greased cake tin.

5. Place the cake tin in the oven. Bake until a toothpick inserted into the centre comes out clean (see page 12), 28 to 32 minutes.

!! 6. Use oven gloves to remove the cake tin from the oven and place it on the hob or a cooling rack. Let the cake cool in the tin for 20 minutes. Using oven gloves, turn the cake out of the tin (see page 15) and let cool completely on the cooling rack.

7. While the cake cools, make the icing: In a medium bowl, whisk together the softened cream cheese, icing sugar, vanilla, water, and pinch of salt until smooth, about 1 minute.

8. Transfer the cake to a serving plate. Use a butter knife or offset spatula to spread the icing over the top of the cake. Cut into slices and serve.

Ingredients

Cake

Vegetable oil spray

2 large eggs, at room temperature

120 ml vegetable oil

60 ml buttermilk

200 g granulated sugar

¼ teaspoon table salt

125 g plain flour

¾ teaspoon bicarbonate of soda

¾ teaspoon baking powder

½ teaspoon ground cinnamon

¼ teaspoon ground ginger

1 medium courgette, grated and gently squeezed to drain

60 g chopped pecans

Icing

115 g full-fat cream cheese, softened (see page 11)

120 g icing sugar

½ teaspoon vanilla extract

2 tablespoons water

Pinch of table salt

SERVES 1

CHOCOLATE-PEANUT BUTTER MUG CAKE

INGREDIENTS

- 30 g unsalted butter, cut into 1-tablespoon pieces
- 2 tablespoons dark chocolate chips
- 1 large egg
- 2 tablespoons granulated sugar
- 1 tablespoon unsweetened Dutch-processed cocoa powder
- ½ teaspoon vanilla extract
- Pinch of table salt
- 2 tablespoons plain flour
- ¼ teaspoon baking powder
- 1 tablespoon smooth peanut butter

Mug cakes come together so quickly they feel almost like magic. Once you start heating the batter, you have to wait for only three minutes before it's ready to dig into. Chocolate and peanut butter are a classic duo. If peanut butter isn't your thing, create your own classic with a different nut butter. If you'd like a little something extra, try adding a scoop of vanilla ice cream or some whipped cream at the end.

1. In a **medium microwave-safe bowl**, combine the butter and chocolate chips. Microwave at 100 per cent power for 1 minute. Use a **silicone spatula** to stir the chocolate mixture. Return to the microwave and microwave at 100 per cent power until melted, about 1 minute longer. Stir until smooth.

2. Add the egg, sugar, cocoa powder, vanilla, and salt to the chocolate mixture and **whisk** until smooth. Add the flour and baking powder and whisk until just combined and no dry flour remains.

3. Use a **spoon** to transfer half of the batter to a **340 ml microwave-safe mug**. Spoon the peanut butter onto the top of the batter in the mug. Layer the rest of the batter on top of the peanut butter (no need to spread it out).

4. Place the mug in the centre of the microwave. Microwave at 50 per cent power until the cake has risen but is still wet on the edges, 1½ to 2 minutes.

!5. Use **oven gloves** to remove the mug from the microwave. Let cool for 1 minute, then enjoy!

YOU'RE THE CHEF!
"This is such a special treat for when you feel like homemade dessert but don't want to make a full recipe. The peanut butter is a fun and creamy surprise in the middle." –Remi, 8

LEMON POUND CAKE

SERVES 8 TO 10

A pound cake is traditionally made with 450 g (1 pound) each of flour, butter, sugar, and eggs (which makes a lot of cake!). This version is scaled down, and the ratios have been changed a bit, but the cake still has a lovely dense, buttery texture much like the original, plus it has a tangy, lemony flavour. Make sure that your loaf tin is at least 23 by 13 cm (9 by 5 in), as the batter will overflow in a smaller tin. Since mixing the melted butter into the batter works best when the butter is still hot, we suggest melting the butter in a measuring jug so you can easily pour it through the funnel of the food processor.

INGREDIENTS

Cake
Vegetable oil spray
280 g plain flour
2 teaspoons baking powder
¼ teaspoon bicarbonate of soda
1 teaspoon table salt
330 g granulated sugar
250 g sour cream
3 large eggs
2 tablespoons grated lemon zest (see page 12)
60 ml fresh lemon juice (see page 12)
1 teaspoon vanilla extract
240 g unsalted butter, melted and kept hot (see page 11)

Glaze
60 g icing sugar
1 tablespoon lemon juice (see page 12)

1. **For the cake:** Set an oven rack in the middle position and heat the oven to 170°C. Generously spray the inside of a **23 by 13 cm (9 by 5 in) metal** or **glass loaf tin** with vegetable oil spray.

2. In a **large bowl**, **whisk** together the flour, baking powder, bicarbonate of soda, and salt.

3. Add the granulated sugar, sour cream, eggs, lemon zest, 60 ml lemon juice, and vanilla to a **food processor**. Lock the lid into place. Process until well mixed, about 10 seconds.

4. With the processor running, pour the hot melted butter through the funnel in a steady stream until incorporated, about 20 seconds. Stop the processor.

!! 5. Remove the processor lid and carefully remove the processor blade. Use a **rubber spatula** to transfer the sugar mixture to the large bowl with the flour mixture.

6. Stir gently until no dry flour remains (make sure to scrape along the bottom and sides of the bowl). Scrape the batter into the greased loaf tin and use the spatula to spread it into an even layer.

7. Place the loaf tin in the oven. Bake until golden brown on top and a **toothpick** inserted into the centre of the cake comes out clean (see page 12), about 1 hour and 15 minutes.

!! 8. Use **oven gloves** to remove the loaf tin from the oven and place it on the hob or a **cooling rack**. Let the cake cool in the tin for 15 minutes.

9. Using oven gloves, turn the cake out of the loaf tin (see page 15). Turn the cake upright on the rack and let it continue to cool completely, at least 1½ hours.

10. **For the glaze:** Transfer the cake to a **serving platter** or **chopping board**. In a **small bowl**, use a **spoon** to stir together the icing sugar and 1 tablespoon lemon juice until smooth. The glaze should drizzle slowly from the spoon. If it's too thick, stir in more lemon juice ½ teaspoon at a time. If it's too thin, add more icing sugar a teaspoon at a time. Use the spoon to spread the glaze all over the top of the cake and let it drip down the sides a little bit. Let the glaze set for at least 10 minutes. Slice and serve.

LEMON-POPPY SEED POUND CAKE

After mixing the batter in step 6, gently stir in 50 g poppy seeds before transferring the batter to the loaf tin.

REBEL IN THE KITCHEN

Pound cakes have long been a staple of bake sales. After Rosa Parks refused to give up her seat on the bus in Alabama and the Montgomery Bus Boycott was underway, chef and activist Georgia Gilmore contributed her cooking skills to the cause. She sold fish and chicken dinners, stewed greens, sweet potato pies, and pound cakes to raise money to hire Black drivers, buy petrol, and pay for car insurance to keep the protest going strong.

MEET CHEF RACHEL GURJAR

Growing up in Mumbai, India, Rachel learned about cooking from her mother. In one of her earliest kitchen memories, she helps peel mangoes as her mother pickles fruits and vegetables on a hot summer afternoon. Their home didn't have an oven, so her mother would "bake" cakes in a pressure cooker. To this day, the smell of her mother's pressure cooker ghee cake takes her back to her childhood — to where she tries to be patient, waiting to dig in to the first warm slice of cake.

In college, Rachel studied journalism. She tried her hand at public relations but knew it wasn't the job for her. After some soul searching, she packed her bags and headed for culinary school in the United States. While in school, she tried all sorts of jobs in the hospitality industry: barista, waiter, host, line cook, prep cook, private chef, caterer, and more. After graduating, she explored food media as a photographer, food writer and editor, and recipe developer. Her social media presence grew and grew.

Rachel enjoys using new ingredients to create fresh takes on the classics she grew up eating. She would like young chefs to know that they don't need a ton of specific ingredients to create a delicious recipe. Instead, she says, you need technique and a basic understanding of flavours. So learn what you can and enjoy being creative in the kitchen!

If Rachel could invite any three women from history to dinner, she would pick Indian freedom fighter Rani Lakshimi Bai, abolitionist Harriet Tubman, and Supreme Court Justice Ruth Bader Ginsburg. She says, "I would make them regional foods from my community: dal baati, bharta, churma, gulab jamun, and kheer."

STRAWBERRY SNACKING CAKE

SERVES 6 TO 8

"Juicy fresh strawberries are cooked down into a quick jam, which is then baked into a soft but crumbly cake. Calling for just minimal prep, this snacking cake is super easy to make and yields a fun and fruity dessert perfect for any occasion. Strawberries are my favourite fruit, and I do not miss an opportunity to include them in simple desserts like this one. Make the jam a few days in advance for an even quicker baking experience. Be sure to zest the lemon – the zest goes into the cake batter – before you juice it for the jam, which you make first. You can store the cake at room temperature, loosely covered with cling film to keep it from drying out, for up to three days. To reheat the cake for serving, place it on a microwave-safe plate and heat it in the microwave for 10 seconds. This cake is delicious on its own, but you can serve it with ice cream and any leftover jam if you'd like." –Rachel Gurjar

1. **For the jam:** Add the strawberries, 55 g sugar, cornflour, lemon juice, and pinch of table salt to a **small saucepan**. Place the pan on the hob and bring the mixture to a boil over medium-low heat. Cook, stirring occasionally with a **wooden spoon**, until some strawberries have disintegrated and the jam is syrupy, 8 to 10 minutes. Turn off the hob and slide the saucepan to a cool part of the hob. Let the jam cool completely, about 30 minutes. If you'd like to make the cake later in the day or on another day, transfer the jam to an airtight container and chill in the fridge until ready to use.

2. **For the cake:** Set an oven rack in the middle position and heat the oven to 180°C. Lightly grease the inside of an **20 cm (8 in) square metal cake tin** with butter. Fit the greased cake tin with a **parchment paper** sling (see page 13).

3. In a **medium bowl**, **whisk** together the flour, polenta, baking powder, and ½ teaspoon table salt. Add the 330 g sugar to the bowl of a **stand mixer** fitted with the **paddle attachment** or to a **large bowl** if you're using a **handheld mixer**. Sprinkle the lemon zest over the sugar. Then use your fingers to rub

INGREDIENTS

Strawberry Jam

450 g fresh strawberries, hulled and cut into 2.5 cm (1 in) pieces (see page 125)

55 g granulated sugar

1 teaspoon cornflour

1 tablespoon fresh lemon juice (see page 12)

Pinch of table salt

Cake

240 g unsalted butter, at room temperature, plus more for greasing

190 g plain flour

75 g yellow stone-ground polenta (cornmeal)

1 teaspoon baking powder

½ teaspoon table salt

330 g granulated sugar

1 teaspoon grated lemon zest (see page 12)

continued

CAKES AND CUPCAKES

95

STRAWBERRY SNACKING CAKE
CONTINUED

the sugar and lemon zest together until evenly combined. Add the butter and beat on medium speed until light and fluffy, 2 to 3 minutes. Stop the mixer and scrape down the sides of the bowl with a **rubber spatula**.

4. With the mixer on low speed, add the eggs one at a time, beating after each addition until incorporated. Then add the vanilla and beat until incorporated, about 10 seconds. Stop the mixer and scrape down the sides of the bowl.

5. With the mixer on low speed, gradually beat in the flour mixture. As you work, stop the mixer as needed and use the spatula to scrape down the sides of the bowl. Add the milk and beat on low speed until combined, about 1 minute. Stop the mixer.

6. Remove the paddle or beaters and scrape any batter sticking to them into the bowl. Stir with the spatula to combine with the rest of the batter.

7. Scrape the batter into the prepared cake tin and use the spatula to smooth the top. Use a **small spoon** to dollop the jam onto the surface of the batter. Use a **butter knife** or **small offset spatula** to swirl the jam gently into the batter.

8. Place the tin in the oven. Bake the cake until the top is golden and a toothpick inserted into the centre comes out clean (see page 12), 55 to 60 minutes.

!! 9. Use **oven gloves** to remove the cake tin from the oven and place it on the hob or a **cooling rack**. Let the cake cool in the tin for 20 minutes. The cake will have slightly crispy edges, and that's normal. Holding the edges of the parchment sling, lift the cake out of the tin and place on a **serving plate**. Slice and serve warm or at room temperature.

---

2 large eggs, at room temperature

1 teaspoon vanilla extract

175 ml whole milk, at room temperature

CAKES AND CUPCAKES

SERVES 8 TO 10

ORANGE SEMOLINA CAKE

Ingredients

Cake
Vegetable oil spray

370 ml whole milk-plain yoghurt

1 tablespoon bicarbonate of soda

375 g semolina flour

200 g granulated sugar

1 tablespoon grated orange zest (see page 12)

½ teaspoon table salt

180 g unsalted butter, melted and cooled (see page 11)

Syrup
110 g granulated sugar

120 ml water

1 orange, cut into 5 mm (¼ in) thick slices

Semolina is used in countries around the world, particularly in the Mediterranean and Middle East, to make foods like couscous, pasta, and an array of cakes, from namoura to basbousa to revani. One thing these cakes all have in common is that they are soaked in a flavourful syrup that is poured over the top while the cake is still hot. Semolina is a type of flour made from durum (a species of wheat), which is milled to a coarser grain than plain flour. This cake is delicious topped with chopped nuts, or, less traditionally, with a dollop of whipped cream (see page 17).

1. **For the cake:** Set an oven rack in the middle position and heat the oven to 190°C. Line the bottom of a **23 cm (9 in) round cake tin** with **parchment paper** (see page 14). Lightly spray the parchment and sides of the tin with vegetable oil spray.

2. In a **medium bowl**, combine the yoghurt and bicarbonate of soda and use a **spoon** to stir just until mixed. Set aside until the mixture has risen slightly and small bubbles appear on the surface, about 10 minutes.

3. In a **large bowl**, **whisk** together the semolina, 200 g sugar, orange zest, and salt until well combined.

4. Add the risen yoghurt mixture and the butter to the semolina mixture and use a **rubber spatula** to stir just until combined. Scrape the batter into the parchment-lined cake tin and use the spatula to spread it into an even layer.

5. Place the cake tin in the oven. Bake until the cake is golden brown on top and a **toothpick** inserted into the centre comes out clean (see page 12), 30 to 35 minutes.

6. While the cake is baking, make the syrup: In a **small saucepan**, combine the 110 g sugar, the water, and orange slices. Place the saucepan on the hob over medium heat. Cook, stirring occasionally and lightly mashing the orange slices with a **wooden spoon**, until the mixture comes to a simmer (small bubbles appear all over the surface) and the sugar is dissolved, 5 to 7 minutes. Turn off the hob and slide the saucepan to a cool part of the hob. Let the syrup cool completely.

!! 7 Use **oven gloves** to remove the cake tin from the oven and place it on the hob or a **cooling rack**. Let the cake cool in the tin for 5 minutes.

!! 8 Set a **fine-mesh sieve** over a **small bowl** or **liquid measuring jug** and carefully strain the orange syrup. Discard the orange slices.

!! 9 Use a **toothpick** or **skewer** to poke holes all over the top of the cake. Be careful, as the cake will still be hot. Drizzle the orange syrup evenly over the surface of the cake, then leave the cake to cool completely, about 1 hour.

!! 10 When the cake has cooled, use a **butter knife** to loosen the edges of the cake from the tin. Place a **large plate** or **serving platter** upside down on top of the cake tin, flip the tin and plate over together, and set the plate on the worktop. Lift the tin off the cake and set aside. Peel off the parchment. Cut the cake into wedges and serve.

YOU'RE THE CHEF!

"This cake was really, really yummy! I added sliced oranges and it made it really pretty. I ate it with vanilla ice cream for dessert. I also had some for breakfast!" —Viva, 12

MEET CHEF NADIYA HUSSAIN

Nadiya grew up in the United Kingdom with two parents and five siblings in a bustling Bangladeshi household. Her mum mostly handled the cooking, sometimes whipping up as many as eight curries a day.

Nadiya started cooking when she was nine years old. Her baking adventures began later. As a newlywed, she started making all sorts of cakes. She loved to watch cooking competitions. "You can do that!" her husband would say. Nadiya, who struggles with a panic disorder, thought he was being completely ridiculous. She could never go on TV!

One day, he brought home an application for *The Great British Bake Off*. He had even filled in some of the answers for her. She completed the application just so he would quit bugging her about it. A few interviews later, Nadiya found herself competing on the hugely popular TV show. And she won!

Through shocked and happy tears, Nadiya said, "I am never ever going to put boundaries on myself ever again. I'm never going to say 'I can't do it' . . . I can. And I will."

Seemingly overnight, she became a well-known cookbook author and TV personality.

Nadiya describes her food as "a mash-up of cultures". She says, "I take the recipes I grew up with and then use elements of British food and put them together in a way that is harmonious".

When Nadiya was a child, her family cooked everything on the hob. She used the oven for the first time when she was 12 years old!

Pear and Cardamom Loaf Cake

Serves 8 to 10

"This is a delicious cake, soft and sweet with a row of tender pears along its centre. Crushed cardamom runs through the batter, scenting it perfectly. I like to serve this cake warm with custard sauce or cream spooned over each slice, but it is also wonderful without any further adornment. You will have some leftover pear halves, which are lovely as a snack or in a smoothie!" —Nadiya Hussain

1. **For the cake:** Set an oven rack in the middle position and heat the oven to 180°C. Fit a **23 by 13 cm (9 by 5 in) loaf tin** with a **parchment paper** sling (see page 13) and spray with vegetable oil spray.

2. Use a **medium fine-mesh sieve** to sift the flour into a **medium bowl**. Add the cardamom and baking powder and **whisk** to mix well.

3. Rinse the sieve. Pour the tin of pears into the sieve held over the sink to drain. Place the pears on a **medium plate** and pat the halves dry with **kitchen towels**. You will need four halves. Save the rest of the halves as a snack or for another use.

4. Add the butter and brown sugar to the bowl of a **stand mixer** fitted with the **paddle attachment** or to a **large bowl** if using a **handheld mixer**. Beat on medium-high speed until the mixture is light and fluffy, about 3 minutes. Stop the mixer and use a **rubber spatula** to scrape down the sides of the bowl.

5. With the mixer running on low speed, add the eggs one at a time, beating after each addition until incorporated. Stop the mixer and scrape down the sides of the bowl.

6. Add the flour mixture and beat on medium speed until the batter is glossy and no dry flour remains, about 1 minute.

7. Arrange the four pear halves, cut side down, in a single row down the centre of the parchment-lined loaf tin.

8. Transfer the batter to the tin. Tap the tin on the worktop a few times to level the surface of the batter.

Ingredients

Cake

Vegetable oil spray

210 g self-raising flour

8 green cardamom pods, crushed, pods discarded, and seeds ground, or ½ teaspoon ground cardamom

1 teaspoon baking powder

420 g tin pear halves in juice

240 g unsalted butter, softened (see page 11)

185 g dark brown sugar

4 large eggs

Glaze

2 tablespoons icing sugar

1 teaspoon vanilla extract

1 tablespoon water, plus more as needed

CONTINUED

PEAR AND CARDAMOM LOAF CAKE
CONTINUED

9. Place the loaf tin in the oven. Bake until the top of the cake is golden, the pears are fully enveloped by the batter, and a toothpick inserted into the centre of the cake comes out with a few moist crumbs attached (see page 12), about 1 hour.

10. **While the cake bakes, make the glaze:** Add the icing sugar, vanilla, and 1 tablespoon of water to a small bowl. Whisk to combine, adding ½ teaspoon water at a time if too thick or ½ teaspoon icing sugar at a time if too runny. You want a glaze that is fluid but not watery.

!! 11. Use oven gloves to remove the loaf tin from the oven and place on the hob or a cooling rack. Let the cake cool in the tin for 1 hour.

12. Use a butter knife to loosen the edges of the cake from the tin. Use the edges of the parchment sling to pull the cake out of the tin. Remove the parchment and place the cake on a serving plate. Drizzle the glaze evenly over the top. Slice and serve.

> Recipe ideas often come to Nadiya in the middle of the night. She doesn't want to wake up the entire house at 3:00 a.m., so she keeps a little notebook by her bed where she can jot down her great ideas.

SERVES 8 TO 10

FLOURLESS CHOCOLATE CAKE

This cake is perfect for the ultimate chocolate fan. Without the flour, the chocolate takes centre stage, making this a gooey and fudgy dessert. Top it with whipped cream or vanilla ice cream for a fancy-looking treat.

INGREDIENTS

Vegetable oil spray

175 g dark chocolate chips

120 g unsalted butter, cut into 8 equal pieces

165 g granulated sugar

1 teaspoon baking powder

¼ teaspoon table salt

4 large eggs

50 g unsweetened Dutch-processed cocoa powder

Whipped cream or vanilla ice cream, for serving (optional)

1. Set an oven rack in the middle position and heat the oven to 180°C. Line the bottom of a **23 cm (9 in) round cake tin** with **parchment paper** (see page 14). Lightly spray the parchment and the tin sides with vegetable oil spray.

2. In a **large microwave-safe bowl**, combine the chocolate chips and butter. Microwave at 100 per cent power for 1 minute. Use a **silicone spatula** to stir the chocolate. Return the bowl to the microwave and microwave at 100 per cent power until melted, 30 seconds to 1 minute longer. Remove the bowl from the microwave and stir with the spatula until the chocolate is fully melted and smooth.

3. Add the sugar, baking powder, salt, and eggs to the bowl with the chocolate mixture and **whisk** until well mixed. Add the cocoa powder and whisk just until combined.

4. Use the spatula to transfer the batter to the prepared cake tin and smooth the top into an even layer. Place the cake tin in the oven. Bake until the top is dry and a **toothpick** inserted into the centre of the cake comes out clean (see page 12), 35 to 45 minutes.

5. Use **oven gloves** to remove the cake tin from the oven and place it on the hob or a **cooling rack**. Let the cake cool in the tin for 30 minutes.

6. Turn the cake out of the tin (see page 15). Turn the cake upright and place on a **serving plate**. Cut into wedges. Serve with whipped cream or ice cream, if desired.

FUN FOOD FACT

La torta tenerina is a type of flourless (or mostly flourless) chocolate cake served in Italy. It is also called the Queen of Montenegro because it was served to Princess Elena of Montenegro when she married Prince Victor Emmanuel III in 1896. When Victor's father died in 1900, he became the king of Italy and Elena became the queen! Some say the sweet, soft centre of the cake was just like Elena's tender heart.

Alana never liked olives until she tried green Castelvetrano olives warmed in olive oil with lemon zest and garlic. Then she went from avoiding them to craving them.

Alana was born and raised in Hawai'i, and she still loves nothing more than making and enjoying local dishes. Food in Hawai'i has been influenced by many cultures over the years. Chinese, Japanese, Portuguese, Filipino, and other cuisines have mixed and mingled with native Hawaiian traditions. Alana's recipes explore these flavours.

In her book, *Aloha Kitchen*, readers will find such dishes as saimin, a popular noodle soup; loco moco, which is a burger patty topped with brown gravy and a fried egg served over rice; and delicious pink guava cake. The book also includes a recipe for one of Alana's favourite dishes: mochiko chicken, which is a marinated and fried chicken that her mum taught her to make. "Whenever I have it," she says, "I think of my school field trips because that's usually when she'd make it for me. She would make me a bento box with that, a triangle musubi, and a Capri-Sun!"

Alana wants young chefs to know that there's no such thing as a failure in the kitchen. "Every dish betters you as a cook," she says. "The more you cook, the better you cook."

If Alana could throw a dinner party with any historical guest, she would invite Queen Lili'uokalani, the last monarch of the kingdom of Hawai'i. She'd make shoyu chicken, ahi poke, pohole fern salad, and a big pot of rice "to show her what local Hawai'i food looks like today".

Chocolate Chip Mochi Muffins

MAKES 12 MUFFINS

"Think of mochi muffins as the bouncier, chewier cousin of traditional muffins (and also as an adaptation of the sweet Hawai'i treat known as butter mochi). They are made with mochiko, or sweet rice flour, so you don't have to worry about overmixing because the flour is naturally gluten-free, which means there's no gluten to make the batter stiff. Make sure to take your eggs out of the fridge at least an hour ahead of time so they can get to room temperature. This will help make combining the eggs with the batter much easier than if they're cold. Pro tip: Be sure to give the tin of coconut milk a good shake, shake, shake before opening it. This ensures the creamier part mixes with the watery liquid." –Alana Kysar

Ingredients

Vegetable oil spray

400 g tin full-fat coconut milk

110 g granulated sugar

95 g light brown sugar

60 g unsalted butter, melted and cooled (see page 11)

2 large eggs, at room temperature

2 teaspoons vanilla extract

220 g mochiko (sweet rice flour)

1½ teaspoons baking powder

½ teaspoon kosher salt

175 g plus 45 g mini chocolate chips, measured separately

1. Set an oven rack in the middle position and heat the oven to 180°C. Spray the inside of each hole of a *12-hole standard muffin tin* well with vegetable oil spray.

2. In a *large bowl*, *whisk* together the coconut milk, granulated sugar, brown sugar, melted butter, eggs, and vanilla until well mixed. Add the mochiko, baking powder, and salt and whisk until smooth. Using a *rubber spatula*, fold 175 g of the chocolate chips into the batter and stir until they are evenly distributed.

3. Divide the batter evenly among the prepared muffin holes. Sprinkle the remaining 45 g chocolate chips on the tops of the muffins, dividing the chips evenly.

4. Tap the muffin tin on the worktop a few times to bring any air bubbles in the batter to the surface.

5. Place the muffin tin in the oven. Bake until the tops are golden brown and a *toothpick* inserted into the centre of a muffin comes out clean (see page 12), 35 to 40 minutes.

!! 6. Use *oven gloves* to remove the muffin tin from the oven and place it on the hob or a *cooling rack*. Let the muffins cool in the tin for at least 20 minutes.

7. Use an *offset spatula* or *butter knife* to carefully release the muffins from their wells. Serve slightly warm or let cool completely before serving.

TRES LECHES DE COCO

SERVES 12 TO 15

INGREDIENTS

Vegetable oil spray

280 g plain flour

2 teaspoons baking powder

1 teaspoon table salt

250 ml whole milk

120 g unsalted butter, cut into 1-tablespoon pieces

2 teaspoons plus 1 teaspoon vanilla extract, measured separately

4 large eggs

400 g granulated sugar

400 g tin sweetened condensed milk

400 g tin full-fat coconut milk

350 g tin evaporated milk

40 g desiccated coconut

1 recipe Whipped Cream (page 17), or canned whipped cream

In Spanish, the phrase *tres leches* means "three milks". Tres leches is a traditional Latin American cake that is typically soaked in three different types of milk: evaporated milk, sweetened condensed milk, and double cream or whole milk. This version offers a tropical twist by using canned coconut milk in place of the double cream or whole milk. (If you want to make a traditional Pastel de Tres Leches, see page 112.) Plan ahead! This cake needs to soak in its milk mixture for at least 3 hours and up to overnight before serving. It's easiest to make this a two-day project, baking the cake on the first day, soaking it overnight, and topping and serving it the next day.

1. Set an oven rack to the middle position and heat the oven to 170°C. Lightly spray the inside of a **23 by 33 cm (9 by 13 in) metal baking tin** with vegetable oil spray.

2. In a **medium bowl**, **whisk** together the flour, baking powder, and salt. Set aside.

3. ⚠ In a **microwave-safe jug**, combine the whole milk and butter pieces. Microwave at 100 per cent power until the milk is warm and the butter is melted, 3 to 4 minutes, stopping and stirring with a **spoon** halfway through. Add 2 teaspoons of the vanilla to the mixture and set aside. Use **oven gloves** to remove the jug from the microwave and place on the worktop.

4. Add the eggs to the bowl of a **stand mixer** fitted with the **whisk attachment** or to a **large bowl** if you're using a **handheld mixer**. If you're using a handheld mixer, place a **damp kitchen towel** underneath the bowl to keep it from moving around as you beat. Beat on medium speed until the eggs are foamy, about 2 minutes. Stop the mixer.

5. Add the sugar to the eggs. Beat the mixture on medium speed until it is pale yellow and thick, about 5 minutes.

6. Reduce the speed to low. With the mixer running, slowly pour in the warm milk mixture and mix until combined, about 30 seconds. Stop the mixer.

7 Add half of the flour mixture. Beat on low speed until combined, about 30 seconds. Stop the mixer. Add the remaining flour mixture and then beat on low speed until fully combined, about 30 more seconds. Stop the mixer. Remove the whisk or beaters and use a **rubber spatula** to scrape any batter sticking to them into the bowl.

8 Use the spatula to stir the batter to make sure no dry flour remains (make sure to scrape along the bottom and sides of the bowl). Scrape the batter into the greased baking tin.

9 Place the baking tin in the oven. Bake until the cake is golden brown on top and a **toothpick** inserted into the centre comes out clean (see page 12), 40 to 45 minutes.

!! 10 Use oven gloves to remove the baking tin from the oven and place it on the hob or a **cooling rack**. Let the cake cool in the tin for 15 minutes.

11 Meanwhile, in a **large measuring jug**, **whisk** together the sweetened condensed milk, coconut milk, evaporated milk, and the remaining 1 teaspoon vanilla.

12 Use a **wooden skewer** to poke holes all over the warm cake, spacing them about 1 cm (½ in) apart. Very slowly drizzle the milk mixture all over the cake until it is completely absorbed. You may need to stop a few times and let it soak in a bit before adding more.

13 Let the cake sit at room temperature for 15 minutes, then chill in the fridge uncovered for at least 3 hours or up to overnight.

14 Thirty minutes before you plan to serve the cake, remove it from the fridge so it can warm slightly.

!! 15 While the cake is warming up, spread the desiccated coconut into an even layer on a **microwave-safe plate**, breaking up any clumps with your hands. Microwave at 100 per cent power until the coconut turns light golden brown, stopping and stirring with a **spoon** every 1 minute. Use **oven gloves** to remove the plate from the microwave (be careful, as the plate will be hot!) and set aside to cool, at least 10 minutes.

CONTINUED

TRES LECHES DE COCO
CONTINUED

16 If you're making the whipped cream, whip it to soft peaks. Use an **offset spatula** or **spoon** to spread the whipped cream evenly over the top of the cake. Then sprinkle the cooled coconut evenly over the cream. Cut the cake into pieces and serve.

PASTEL DE TRES LECHES

Add ½ teaspoon ground cinnamon to the flour mixture in step 2. Use 250 ml double cream in place of the coconut milk in step 11. Skip the toasted coconut on top and sprinkle lightly with ground cinnamon.

 **FUN FOOD FACT**

Coconut is used in lots of different types of sweets. Beloved painter Frida Kahlo counted coconut-stuffed limes among her favourite desserts. She also painted coconuts in her still lifes.

SERVES 8 TO 10

COFFEE CRUMB CAKE

INGREDIENTS

Vegetable oil spray

125 g plain flour

150 g granulated sugar

¾ teaspoon baking powder

¼ teaspoon bicarbonate of soda

1 teaspoon ground cinnamon

¼ teaspoon table salt

250 ml whole milk

1 large egg

1 teaspoon vanilla extract

90 g unsalted butter, melted and cooled (see page 11)

1 recipe Crumble (page 116)

1 teaspoon icing sugar, for dusting

Don't worry, there's no coffee in this cake! Coffee cake gets its name from being a cake that's great to have alongside a hot drink, particularly coffee. It's believed that this idea of pairing a treat with your coffee was introduced to the United States by German immigrants in the 1800s who wanted to continue their tradition of Kaffeezeit, a daily afternoon break with friends and family at which a baked good and coffee are enjoyed. This recipe is based on American coffee cake, which has many different versions that include ingredients like actual coffee, sour cream, and nuts. If you were to participate in Kaffeezeit while in Germany, you wouldn't see *this* cake there, but you might spot similar-looking goodies.

1 Set an oven rack in the middle position and heat the oven to 180°C. Spray the inside of a 23 cm (9 in) round cake tin with vegetable oil spray. Line the cake tin with a circle of parchment paper (see page 14).

2 In a large bowl, whisk together the flour, granulated sugar, baking powder, bicarbonate of soda, cinnamon, and salt until combined. Add the milk, egg, vanilla, and melted butter and stir with a rubber spatula until combined and no dry flour remains.

3 Transfer half of the batter to the greased cake tin and use the spatula to spread it into an even layer. Use your hands to sprinkle half of the crumble topping over the surface of the batter. Use a butter knife to swirl the crumble gently into the batter.

4 Transfer the remainder of the batter to the cake tin. Sprinkle the remaining crumble topping evenly over the top.

5 Place the cake tin in the oven. Bake until the centre of the cake looks set and a toothpick inserted into the centre comes out with a few moist crumbs attached (see page 12), 30 to 35 minutes.

!! 6 Use oven gloves to remove the cake tin from the oven and place it on the hob or a cooling rack. Let the cake cool completely in the tin, about 1 hour.

CONTINUED

COFFEE CRUMB CAKE
CONTINUED

7 Use a **fine-mesh sieve** to dust the top of the cooled cake with the icing sugar (see page 16). Cut into wedges and serve.

CRUMBLE

In a **medium bowl**, **whisk** together 90 g melted butter, 45 g brown sugar, 1 teaspoon ground cinnamon, and ¼ teaspoon table salt until well mixed. Add 125 g plain flour and use a **rubber spatula** to stir until clumps begin to form. If there are any large clumps, use your fingers to break them up into pea-sized pieces. Set aside until ready to use.

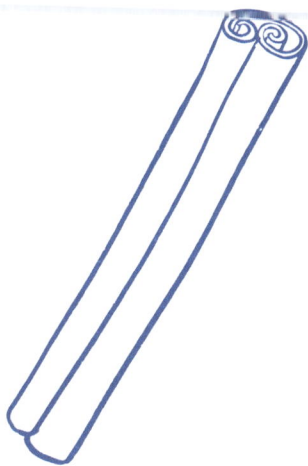

 REBEL IN THE KITCHEN

Irma Rombauer's famous (and famously chatty) cookbook, *The Joy of Cooking*, came out in the USA in 1923. Irma's family was from Germany, and she included in the book many recipes that were popular in Germany, such as blitzkuchen, a type of coffee cake, and a Linzer torte, which is a dessert consisting of buttery, nutty pastry and fruit preserves. About the Linzer torte she wrote, "The German recipe reads, 'stir for one hour,' but, of course, no high-gear American has time for that."

NO-BAKE CHEESECAKE
with Any-Biscuit Crust

SERVES 10 TO 12

Plan ahead! This no-bake cheesecake needs to chill in the fridge for at least 6 hours or up to overnight before you can slice and serve it. Homemade whipped cream will make this cheesecake extra light and airy, but if you're short on time, shop-bought canned whipped cream will work fine. If using canned whipped cream, place it in the fridge a couple of hours before making this recipe for the right consistency.

1. **For the crust:** Add the cookies to the bowl of a **food processor** and lock the lid into place. Process until the cookies break down into fine crumbs, 15 to 30 seconds. Stop the processor.

!!2. Remove the processor lid and carefully remove the processor blade. Measure out 225 g crumbs. Rinse and dry the food processor bowl before making the cheesecake filling.

3. In a **medium bowl**, use a **rubber spatula** to stir together the cookie crumbs, 2 tablespoons sugar, and salt. Add 3 tablespoons of the melted butter and stir until the crumbs are evenly moistened.

4. Pinch some of the crumbs together with your fingers. If the crumbs hold their shape in a clump and feel like wet sand, you're all set. If they're dry and crumbly, keep stirring in more melted butter, 1 tablespoon at a time, until the crumbs stick together. (The amount of butter you need will vary depending on the type of cookie you're using.)

5. Tip the crumbs into a **23 cm (9 in) springform tin** and use the spatula to spread them into an even layer. Use the bottom of a dry mug or glass to press the crumb-butter mixture evenly onto the bottom and up the sides of the tin. You'll have to go around a few times to get the crumbs firmly and evenly shaped. Place the tin in the freezer for at least 15 minutes.

6. **While the crust is in the freezer, make the filling:** Add the softened cream cheese and 75 g sugar to a food processor bowl and lock the lid into place. Process until very smooth with no lumps of cream cheese remaining, 1 to 2 minutes. Stop the processor.

INGREDIENTS

Biscuit Crust

225 g biscuits (like Oreos, Biscoff, or gingersnaps)

2 tablespoons granulated sugar

Pinch of table salt

90 g unsalted butter, melted and cooled (see page 11)

Filling

450 g full-fat cream cheese, cut into 2.5 cm (1 in) pieces and softened (see page 11)

75 g granulated sugar

3 tablespoons sour cream

1 tablespoon fresh lemon juice (see page 12)

½ teaspoon vanilla extract

1 recipe Whipped Cream (page 17), or canned whipped cream

CONTINUED

CAKES AND CUPCAKES

NO-BAKE CHEESECAKE WITH ANY-COOKIE CRUST
CONTINUED

7 Remove the processor lid and scrape down the sides of the bowl with a rubber spatula. Add the sour cream, lemon juice, and vanilla and lock the lid back into place. Process until well combined, about 30 seconds. Stop the processor.

!! 8 Remove the processor lid and carefully remove the processor blade. Use the spatula to scrape the cream cheese mixture into a **large bowl**.

9 If you're making the whipped cream, whip the cream to stiff peaks. Add about one-third of the whipped cream to the bowl with the cream cheese mixture. Using the rubber spatula, gently stir together until well mixed. Add the remaining whipped cream on top. Using the spatula, cut downwards through the mixture to the bottom of the bowl, then scrape along the bottom and up the side closest to you, scooping the mixture from the bottom and folding it over the top. Rotate the bowl a quarter turn and repeat, cutting downwards, scraping along the bottom and up the side, and folding over the top. Continue until the mixture is just combined but the whipped cream is still fluffy.

10 Remove the springform tin from the freezer. Scrape the cheesecake filling into the tin over the crust and use the spatula to smooth the top. Cover the tin with **cling film** and place it in the fridge. Chill the cheesecake until set, at least 6 hours or up to overnight (the longer, the better).

11 Remove the cake from the fridge and discard the cling film. Use a **butter knife** to carefully loosen the edges of the cake from the sides of the tin. Open the latch on the tin and carefully lift the sides off the cake.

!! 12 Hold a **chef's knife** under hot running water in the sink until the blade is warm. Use the warm knife to cut the cake into slices, wiping the knife with a **clean tea towel** after each cut to keep the slices crumb-free. Serve.

YOU'RE THE CHEF!
"It was really tasty and had that amazing sour-sweet taste that is found in most cheesecakes. It was easier to make than most other cheesecakes." —Maya, 14

DESSERTS

- **123** Blackberry Cobbler
  Any-Berry Cobbler
- **126** Strawberry Shortcakes
- **131** Lebanese-Style Fruit Cocktail
  by Chef Reem Assil
- **132** Peach Melba
- **134** Crêpes Suzette
- **139** Banana Split Bites
  by Chef Chrissy Tracey
- **140** Stuffed Dates

BLACKBERRY COBBLER

SERVES 8

This summery cobbler is extra delicious served with a scoop of vanilla ice cream or a dollop of whipped cream (see page 198 and 17, respectively, to make your own). If you're using frozen berries, you'll need to thaw them and pat them dry first. Here's the easiest way to do this: Line a baking tray with a double layer of kitchen towels. Spread the frozen berries in an even layer on the towel-lined baking tray and let them sit at room temperature for about 20 minutes. Pat them dry with more kitchen towels, and you're good to go!

INGREDIENTS

Vegetable oil spray

420 g fresh blackberries, or thawed if frozen

Grated zest and juice of ½ lemon, kept separate (see page 12)

110 g plus 165 g granulated sugar, measured separately

190 g pain flour

1½ teaspoons baking powder

½ teaspoon table salt

250 ml milk

120 g unsalted butter, melted and cooled (see page 11)

1 teaspoon vanilla extract

1. Set an oven rack in the middle position and heat the oven to 200°C. Spray the inside of an **20 cm (8 in) square** or other **2-litre glass** or **ceramic baking dish** with vegetable oil spray.

2. In a **medium bowl**, combine the blackberries, lemon juice, and 110 g of the sugar. Stir with a **spoon** until the berries are evenly coated with the sugar. Set aside.

3. In a **second medium bowl**, **whisk** together the flour, baking powder, and salt. In a **large bowl**, whisk together the milk, melted butter, vanilla, lemon zest, and the remaining 165 g sugar.

4. Add the flour mixture to the milk mixture and stir with a **rubber spatula** until just combined and no dry flour remains (make sure to scrape along the bottom and sides of the bowl).

5. Scrape the batter into the greased baking dish. Spoon the blackberries and their juice in an even layer on top of the batter. Do not stir them in.

!! 6. Place the baking dish in the oven. Bake until the top of the cobbler is golden brown and the centre doesn't wobble when you shake the dish (holding it with oven gloves, of course!), 35 to 45 minutes.

!! 7. Use **oven gloves** to remove the baking dish from the oven and place it on the hob or a **cooling rack**. Let the cobbler cool in the dish for at least 10 minutes before serving. Serve warm.

CONTINUED

FRUIT DESSERTS

BLACKBERRY COBBLER
CONTINUED

ANY-BERRY COBBLER

Blackberries are the traditional choice for cobblers in the American South, where they grow abundantly, but you can make this cobbler with any berry you like! Try swapping in fresh or frozen raspberries, blueberries, or sliced strawberries, or a mix of your favourite berries.

 ### REBEL IN THE KITCHEN

Edna Lewis was one of the first Black Southern women to publish a cookbook without hiding her race or gender. She wrote lovingly about harvesting and cooking fresh ingredients. She grew up in Freetown, Virginia, where blackberries were plentiful along streams. They ripened around the same time that wheat needed to be harvested. After a long, hard day of threshing wheat, everyone looked forward to a big, juicy blackberry cobbler.

HOW TO HULL STRAWBERRIES

1

Place the washed strawberries on their sides on a **chopping board**. Holding a **paring knife** in your dominant hand (right if you're a righty, left if you're a lefty), cut the white end and green leaves off the strawberry. Repeat with the rest of the berries.

Cut the berries to the size called for in the recipe.

FRUIT DESSERTS

STRAWBERRY SHORTCAKES

SERVES 12

INGREDIENTS

- 450 g fresh strawberries, hulled and roughly chopped (see page 125)
- 2 tablespoons plus 75 g granulated sugar, measured separately
- 190 g plain flour
- 1½ teaspoons baking powder
- ¼ teaspoon bicarbonate of soda
- ¼ teaspoon table salt
- 120 ml whole milk
- 120 g unsalted butter, melted and cooled (see page 11)
- Vegetable oil spray
- 1 recipe Whipped Cream (page 17), or canned whipped cream

These summery shortcakes double up on the strawberry flavour by including pieces of fruit in the shortcake dough. Don't use frozen strawberries here, as they won't hold up well in the filling.

1. Set an oven rack in the middle position and heat the oven to 200°C. Line a **baking tray** with **parchment paper**.

2. In a **medium bowl**, macerate the berries by combining the strawberries and the 2 tablespoons of sugar. Use a **spoon** to gently toss the strawberries until well coated with the sugar. Set aside.

3. In a **large bowl**, **whisk** together the flour, baking powder, bicarbonate of soda, salt, and the remaining 75 g sugar until well mixed.

4. Add the milk, melted butter, and 120 g of chopped strawberries to the bowl with the flour mixture, reserving the remaining strawberries for later. Use a **rubber spatula** to stir until just combined and no dry flour remains.

5. Place 12 equal-sized portions of the dough on the parchment-lined baking tray, spacing them at least 5 cm (2 in) apart.

6. Place the baking tray in the oven. Bake until the shortcakes are browned on top and a **toothpick** inserted into the centre of a shortcake comes out with moist crumbs attached (see page 12), 20 to 25 minutes. If you're making the whipped cream, whip to soft peaks while the shortcakes are baking.

!!7. Use **oven gloves** to remove the baking tray from the oven and place it on the hob or a **cooling rack**. Let the biscuits cool on the tin for 15 minutes.

8. Use a **butter knife** to cut each shortcake in half horizontally (through the middle) so you have a top and bottom for each shortcake. Place each shortcake bottom, cut side up, on an **individual plate**. Top with the remaining macerated strawberries and then the whipped cream, dividing them both evenly. Close with the biscuit tops, cut side down, and serve.

FUN FOOD FACT

Shortcake has been around for a long time! There's a recipe for it in an English cookbook from 1588 called *The Good Huswifes Handmaide for Cookerie in Her Kitchen*. In *The Merry Wives of Windsor*, first published in 1602, William Shakespeare even made a reference to a woman named Alice Shortcake.

Reem loves to eat vegetables, but she didn't love cauliflower until she tried it fried and "dusted with fun spices".

As a "latchkey kid" in the 1990s, Reem would come home from school, let herself in, and be on her own until her parents returned from work. That meant her first kitchen adventures involved simple foods like ramen and mac and cheese. It wasn't until a bit later in life that she leaned into the rich culinary traditions of her parents' home countries, Syria and Palestine.

After 10 years of working as a community and labour organizer, Reem felt unsure of her next move. While travelling with her father through Lebanon and Syria, she realized what she wanted to do. She wanted to combine her passions for social justice, community, and food.

Reem returned to the United States, enrolled in culinary school, and threw herself into learning as much as she could about cooking and running a community-based food business. She sold her incredible baked goods at farmers' markets before opening her first Reem's. Modeled after the Arab corner bakeries she grew up visiting, her restaurants serve fresh-baked bread and beloved dishes like musakhan, chicken brined in sumac with caramelized onions; muhammara, roasted red pepper–walnut dip; and knafeh, a Middle Eastern dessert of sweet cheese and shredded filo dough doused in a flower-flavoured syrup.

In 2022, Reem published the award-winning cookbook *Arabiyya: Recipes from the Life of an Arab in Diaspora*.

Reem describes her signature dishes as "Arab street food made with California love."

LEBANESE-STYLE FRUIT COCKTAIL

SERVES 4

"You can find these fruit refreshments in cafés all over Lebanon. Made with layers of different fruits and textures and topped with clotted cream called ashta and toasted nuts, they are a perfect treat for a hot summer day. In this recipe, I've substituted whipped cream for ashta. Make sure to prep your avocados ahead of time so they have enough time to freeze." —Reem Assil

1. If you're making the whipped cream, whip the cream to soft peaks. Add ⅓ of the whipped cream to a **medium bowl**. Drizzle the orange blossom water over the top. Using a **rubber spatula**, gently stir together the orange blossom water and whipped cream just until mixed. Add the remaining whipped cream on top. Using the spatula, cut downwards through the mixture to the bottom of the bowl, then scrape along the bottom and up the side closest to you, scooping the mixture from the bottom and folding it over the top. Rotate the bowl a quarter turn and repeat, cutting downwards, scraping along the bottom and up the side, and folding over the top. Continue until the mixture is just combined but the whipped cream is still fluffy. Set aside.

2. In a **blender**, combine the avocado, 1 tablespoon of the sugar, and the milk. Put the lid on the blender and hold it in place with a **folded kitchen towel**. Blend to a smooth puree, about 1 minute. Use a **spoon** to divide the avocado puree evenly among **four tall glasses**. Place the glasses in the fridge while you make the other components.

3. Rinse the blender jug, then add the frozen berries and water to it, top with the lid, hold the lid in place with the towel, and blend to a smooth puree as you did the avocado. Stop the blender and check the consistency of the puree. If you would like a thinner consistency, add a little water, top with the lid again, and blend until smooth. Remove the glasses from the fridge and use the spoon to divide the berry puree evenly among them.

4. Top the berry layer with the fruit cubes and/or slices, dividing them evenly among the glasses. Dollop one-fourth of the whipped cream on top of the berry layer in each glass. Sprinkle the cream with the almonds, dividing them evenly, and then drizzle with the honey for the final touch. Enjoy with a **long spoon**.

INGREDIENTS

½ recipe Whipped Cream (page 17), or canned whipped cream

1½ teaspoons orange blossom water

300 g frozen avocado chunks

1 tablespoon plus 1 tablespoon granulated sugar, measured separately

250 ml whole milk

450 g frozen strawberries or mixed berries

175 ml water, plus more as needed

165 g cut-up peeled mango, pineapple, kiwi, or fruit of your choice, in 2.5 cm (1 in) cubes and/or slices

45 g toasted flaked almonds

1 tablespoon honey

SERVES 2

PEACH MELBA

Peach Melba is usually made with poached peaches. To make this classic dessert simpler, we macerate the peaches with sugar, lemon, and vanilla, which softens the peaches and brings out their juices, resulting in a flavour boost without turning on the hob. Here, we use frozen peaches (see the intro paragraph for Blackberry Cobbler, page 123, for the best way to thaw them), but you can substitute ripe fresh peaches. You'll just need to stone and slice them.

INGREDIENTS

125 g fresh raspberries, or thawed if frozen, plus 40 g fresh raspberries, or thawed if frozen (if using frozen, see intro paragraph on page 123), plus more for serving if desired

2 tablespoons, plus 1 tablespoon granulated sugar, measured separately

Pinch of table salt

225 g sliced, frozen peaches, thawed

1 teaspoon fresh lemon juice (see page 12)

½ teaspoon vanilla extract

2 scoops vanilla ice cream, homemade (see page 198) or shop-bought

1. Add the 125 g raspberries, 2 tablespoons granulated sugar, and salt to a **blender**. Put the lid on the blender and hold it in place with a **folded kitchen towel**. Turn on the blender and process until smooth, about 1 minute. Stop the blender.

2. Set a **fine-mesh sieve** over a **jug or bowl**. Pour the raspberry mixture into the strainer. Using a **rubber spatula**, stir and press the mixture to push as much liquid as possible through the sieve into the jug or bowl. Discard any seeds and solids left in the sieve. You can store the sauce in the fridge in an **airtight container** for up to 4 days.

3. In a **medium bowl**, combine the peaches, 1 tablespoon sugar, lemon juice, and vanilla. Use a **spoon** to stir the peaches until they are well coated with the other ingredients. Let the peaches sit at room temperature for 10 minutes.

4. Divide the peaches evenly between **two dessert bowls**. Top each bowl of peaches with half of the 40 g raspberries and a scoop of ice cream.

5. Drizzle the contents of each bowl with 60 ml of the raspberry sauce. Top with more raspberries if you like and serve right away.

YOU'RE THE CHEF!
"It was really good and easy to make. I especially liked the raspberry sauce that was with it. And, of course, the ice cream!" —Arden, 10

SERVES 4

CRÊPES SUZETTE

INGREDIENTS

Sauce
75 ml fresh orange juice (see page 12)
60 g unsalted butter
55 g granulated sugar

Crêpes
175 ml whole milk
2 large eggs
15 g unsalted butter, melted and cooled (see page 11)
½ teaspoon grated orange zest (see page 12)
60 g plain flour
½ teaspoon granulated sugar
¼ teaspoon table salt
½ teaspoon vegetable oil, plus more if needed
Icing sugar, for serving

Crêpes Suzette is a French dessert that is traditionally made with an orange liqueur sauce and is set aflame using a technique called flambéing. To make this classic kid-friendly, we made the sauce with orange juice and skipped the flames. You'll need just one good-sized orange for this recipe, and you'll be using both the zest and the juice, so make sure to zest the fruit before juicing it for the sauce.

1. **For the sauce:** In a **small saucepan**, combine the orange juice, 60 g butter, and 55 g sugar. Place the pan on the hob over medium-high heat and bring to a boil.

2. Turn down the heat to medium-low and simmer (small bubbles appear all over the surface), stirring occasionally with a **wooden spoon**, until the sauce has thickened, 8 to 10 minutes. Turn off the hob and slide the saucepan to a cool part of the hob.

3. **For the crêpes:** Set a **wire rack** inside a **baking tray** and place the setup near the hob. In a **large bowl**, combine the milk, eggs, 15 g melted butter, and orange zest. **Whisk** until blended.

4. Add the flour, ½ teaspoon sugar, and salt to the bowl. Whisk until well mixed and no dry flour remains.

5. Add the vegetable oil to a **25 cm (10 in) nonstick frying pan**. Use a **paper towel** to wipe the inside of the frying pan with the oil until only a thin film remains. Place the frying pan on the hob over medium-low heat and heat for 2 minutes.

6. Use a **measuring jug** to transfer about 60 ml of the batter to the frying pan. Lift the frying pan and carefully tilt and swirl it until the bottom is evenly coated with a thin layer of batter. Then set the pan back on the hob.

7. Turn the heat down to low and cook until the crêpe is set and just beginning to brown on the edges, 1½ to 2 minutes. Slide a **spatula** underneath the crêpe and carefully flip in one quick motion. Continue to cook until the second side is beginning to brown, about 1 minute more. Transfer the crêpe to the prepared wire rack.

8. Repeat steps 6 and 7 to make five more crêpes. If the crêpes begin to stick to the frying pan, add another ½ teaspoon oil to the pan. When all of the crêpes are cooked, turn off the hob and slide the frying pan to a cool part of the hob.

9. Fold each crêpe into quarters. Return the crêpes to the frying pan (some overlap is OK) and pour the sauce on top. Place the frying pan on the hob over medium-low heat and cook until the sauce is bubbling and the crêpes are warmed through, 1 to 2 minutes. Use the spatula to transfer to a **serving plate**. Pour the remaining sauce over the crêpes. Use a **fine-mesh sieve** to dust the crêpes with a little icing sugar (see page 16). Serve.

YOU'RE THE CHEF!
"The crêpes are perfectly soft, fluffy, and soul-filling. The orange-butter sauce is rich and flavourful!" —Luka, 14

One thing Chrissy wishes she had learned earlier in her career was solid knife skills. Great knife skills can help cooks be faster, safer, and more efficient in the kitchen.

Chrissy is a first-generation Jamaican American. When she was a child, she would tag along with her mum on Saturdays as she shopped for imported ingredients at special markets in Manhattan and Brooklyn. She watched as her mother handpicked ackee, callaloo, starfruit, and other fruits and veggies. The next day, her mum would cook, humming a tune as she chopped, stirred, and seasoned her food. Then the family would feast together.

Chrissy learned more than cooking skills from her mother. She learned to cook from the heart. "Cooking is my mother's love language," she says, "and it quickly became mine too".

Chrissy is a vegan chef. "Everything I do is inspired by mushrooms and plants!" she says. Chrissy's grandmother grew up eating dishes like oxtail stew, a flavourful recipe made with butter beans and the beef that comes from the tail of a cow. Later in life, she became a vegetarian. Chrissy didn't want her to miss out on her favourite flavours, so she developed a vegan "oxtail" recipe using a plant protein called vital wheat gluten, which she marinated with Jamaican spices. Her grandmother was thrilled!

Growing up, Chrissy did not see chefs on TV who looked like her. Now, when she sees her name in *Bon Appétit* or opens her book, *Forage & Feast*, she is proud and grateful. She's accomplished more than she ever thought was possible and wants other girls to know they can achieve their dreams as well.

For a long time, Chrissy was not a fan of tofu. But she kept trying it because it is such a good source of plant-based protein. One day, her sister Nikki served her teriyaki tofu, and she was hooked. Now she knows the secrets to making tofu just the way she likes it.

FRUIT DESSERTS

BANANA SPLIT BITES

MAKES 10 TO 12 BANANA BITES

"In my kitchen, I live by the mantra that delicious treats can also nurture our bodies, and this recipe is a vibrant showcase of my philosophy. Imagine taking a bite that's not only sweet but also brimming with the goodness of fresh fruit, dark chocolate, and a little whipped cream and is topped with a gorgeous red cherry – it's nearly perfect! This isn't just food. It's an ode to flavour, the delight of eating well, and the freedom to consume what makes us feel good, both inside and out. After all, balance in all things is the key to living a health-conscious and joyful lifestyle. Enjoy!" —Chrissy Tracey

INGREDIENTS

95 g rainbow sprinkles

85 g dark chocolate chips or shavings or dark chocolate buttons

1 tablespoon extra-virgin olive oil

2 bananas

½ recipe Whipped Cream (page 17), or canned whipped cream

10 to 12 maraschino cherries, for garnish (optional)

1. First, set up your dipping station. Line a **baking tray** with **parchment paper**. Fill a **small bowl** with the sprinkles and place it next to the baking tray.

2. In a **medium microwave-safe bowl**, combine the chocolate chips and oil. Microwave at 50 per cent power for 1 minute. Use a **rubber spatula** to stir the chocolate mixture. Return to the microwave and microwave at 50 per cent power until melted, about 1 minute longer. Stir until smooth.

3. Peel a banana and place it on a **chopping board**. Use a **butter knife** to trim off the pointed ends, then cut the banana on the diagonal into five or six pieces, each 5–7.5 cm (2–3 in) long. Repeat with the second banana.

4. Using a **toothpick** or your hands, and working with one banana piece at a time, dip one side of the piece into the chocolate, letting the excess chocolate drip back into the bowl. Then, moving quickly, dip the chocolate-dipped part of the banana into the sprinkles and set the banana piece on the parchment-lined baking tray. Repeat until all the banana pieces have been dipped in chocolate and coated with sprinkles.

5. Pop the banana pieces into the freezer until firm, about 30 minutes. Once the banana bites are firm, you can transfer them to an **airtight container** or **sealable plastic bag** and store them in the freezer for up to 3 days.

6. To serve, use a **small spoon** to top each banana piece with a tiny dollop of whipped cream, followed by a maraschino cherry (if using). Enjoy immediately!

FRUIT DESSERTS

STUFFED DATES

MAKES 12 DATES

Dates and stuffed dates are often included in iftar, the meal served to break the daily fast during the Islamic holy month of Ramadan, and at the Eid al-Fitr celebrations that occur at the end of Ramadan. The date palm, the tree from which dates are harvested, is mentioned 22 times in the Qu'ran, and breaking the fast with dates was strongly recommended by the Prophet Muhammad.

Pitted dates have a slit cut down their length that you can use to stuff them with filling. If you're using dates that have stones, ask a grown-up to help you use kitchen scissors to cut a slit the long way down the centre of each date. Squeeze out the stone from each date and discard before filling.

INGREDIENTS

- 35 g shelled pistachios
- 60 g almond butter or nut butter of choice
- 2 tablespoons unsweetened desiccated coconut, plus more for sprinkling
- 1 tablespoon honey
- ¼ teaspoon ground cardamom
- Pinch of table salt
- 12 pitted Medjool dates

1. Put the pistachios into a **large sealable plastic bag**, push out all of the air, and seal the bag. Lay the bag flat on a worktop and use a **rolling pin** or **small saucepan** to lightly crush the nuts into small pieces.

2. In a **medium bowl**, combine the crushed pistachios, almond butter, coconut, honey, cardamom, and salt. Use a **rubber spatula** to stir until the ingredients are well mixed.

3. Use a **teaspoon** to scoop a heaped teaspoon of filling into the centre of each date. Place the dates on a **large plate**.

4. Sprinkle the filled dates with coconut. Serve.

FUN FOOD FACT

In Roman times, the dates that grew near the Dead Sea were considered especially tasty. When Cleopatra reigned, King Herod gifted her some treasured date groves. As you snack on these delicious dates, imagine Egypt's last pharaoh eating them too!

PASTRIES,

145	Upside-Down Apple Pastries
146	No-Bake Key Lime Pie Jars
149	Vanillepudding mit Erdbeersoße **by Chef Luisa Weiss**
152	Sour Cream Pastry
154	Dutch Apple Pie
158	Raspberry Fool Rhubarb Fool
161	Mango Cream Pie **by Chef Abi Balingit**
165	Capirotada de Agua
167	Banana Pudding
170	Chocoflan
173	Cherry Galette Cherry Chocolate Galette
176	Lemon Possets
179	Guyanese Pine Tarts
182	Thiakry
185	Guava and Cheese Pastelitos
186	Oat Milk Chocolate Pudding
188	Mango Sago
191	Chocolate Tarte Soleil with Dulce de Leche Dipping Sauce

PUDDINGS, AND PIES

UPSIDE-DOWN APPLE PASTRIES

SERVES 4

These upside-down puff pastries look fancy but are super quick to make! Use apples that hold well when baked, such as Honeycrisp, Granny Smith, or Jonagold. To thaw frozen puff pastry, let it sit in the fridge overnight, or unwrap it and let it sit on the worktop at room temperature until pliable but not too soft, about 30 minutes. These are lovely with a scoop of ice cream on top.

INGREDIENTS

1 Granny Smith, Jonagold, or Honeycrisp apple, cored and sliced 5 mm (¼ in) thick (see page 156)

4 teaspoons brown sugar

¼ teaspoon ground cinnamon

¼ teaspoon table salt

1 (23 cm (9 in) square) sheet puff pastry, thawed

1 large egg

1. Set an oven rack in the middle position and heat the oven to 200°C. Line a **baking tray** with **parchment paper**.

2. Divide the apple slices evenly among the four quarters of the parchment-lined baking tray. You should have four or five slices in each quarter. Arrange the slices in each quarter so they are slightly overlapping one another: the top of one slice is touching the bottom of the next.

3. Add the sugar, cinnamon, and salt to a **small bowl** and mix until combined. Sprinkle a teaspoon of the mixture over each group of apple slices.

!! 4. Unfold the puff pastry on a **chopping board**. Use a **bench scraper** or **chef's knife** to cut the puff pastry into four equal squares.

5. Lay one pastry square over each portion of apple slices, making sure the slices are fully covered by the pastry. Press along the edges against the parchment so no gaps remain between the pastry and the baking tray.

6. Crack the egg into a **small bowl**. Beat lightly with a **fork** until blended. Use a **pastry brush** to paint each pastry square with the beaten egg.

7. Place the baking tray in the oven. Bake until the pastries have risen and are golden brown, 15 to 20 minutes.

!! 8. Use **oven gloves** to remove the baking tray from the oven and place it on the hob or a **cooling rack**. Let the pastries cool on the tray for at least 10 minutes. Use a **spatula** to lift and then flip each pastry over onto a **serving plate**. Serve warm.

SERVES 4

NO-BAKE KEY LIME PIE JARS

INGREDIENTS

60 g digestive biscuit crumbs

1 tablespoon brown sugar

Pinch of table salt

30 g unsalted butter, melted and cooled (see page 11)

115 g full-fat cream cheese, cut into 2.5 cm (1 in) pieces and softened (see page 11)

150 ml sweetened condensed milk

75 ml Key lime juice

2 tablespoons double cream

Grated zest of ½ Persian lime (see page 12)

½ recipe Whipped Cream (page 17), or canned whipped cream

The limes you most often see at the supermarket are called Persian limes. Key limes are a special kind of lime that is much smaller, and their tart, fragrant juice is prized for making Key lime pie. They grow in tropical regions but are delicate and hard to ship. If you can find them fresh, you can use them in this recipe (though you'll need a lot of limes to get 75 ml juice!). Fresh-squeezed Persian lime juice works too. Just don't use bottled Persian lime juice, as it is usually pretty bitter.

1. In a **medium bowl**, use a **rubber spatula** to stir together the digestive biscuit crumbs, brown sugar, and salt. To make the crumbs, grind the biscuits in a food processor or add them to a resealable bag, press out the air, and bash them into fine crumbs with a rolling pin. Add the melted butter and stir until the crumbs are evenly moistened and look like wet sand.

2. Add 2 **tablespoons** of the biscuit crumbs to each of **four 225 g jars**. Swirl each jar to spread the crumbs into an even layer at the bottom. Transfer the remaining crumbs to an **airtight container** and save for serving.

3. Add the softened cream cheese and condensed milk to a **food processor** and lock the lid into place. Process until very smooth with no lumps of cream cheese remaining, 1 to 2 minutes. Stop the processor.

4. Remove the processor lid and scrape down the sides of the bowl with the rubber spatula. Add the lime juice, cream, and lime zest and lock the lid back into place. Process until well mixed, about 30 seconds. Stop the processor.

!!5. Remove the lid and carefully remove the processor blade. Use a **spoon** to divide the Key lime filling evenly among the jars.

6. Cover the jars with **lids** or **cling film** and transfer to the fridge. Chill until firm, at least 1 hour or up to overnight.

7. If you're making the whipped cream, just before you're ready to serve your pie jars, whip the cream to soft peaks. Dollop the cream onto the top of each "pie", then sprinkle the cream with the reserved biscuit crumbs. Serve.

👨‍🍳 REBEL IN THE KITCHEN

In 1983, US President Ronald Reagan invited Maida Heatter, a self-taught baker known as the Queen of Cake, to make 15 Key lime pies for an important economic summit. It was early in the season, and there had recently been a hurricane, so Maida scrambled to find enough Key limes. She spent days visiting everyone she knew with lime trees in their back garden and bartering with fruit vendors until she had enough. But just before her pies could be served to leaders from around the world, the Secret Service dropped them!

MEET CHEF LUISA WEISS

Luisa was born in Berlin, Germany. As a kid, she split her time between Berlin and Brookline, Massachusetts. Her summers were spent with relatives in Italy. And these three countries have influenced her life as a chef and cookbook author.

One of her earliest kitchen memories is of making corn cookies drizzled with chocolate with her friend Joanie. Joanie, who was like a second mother to her, taught her some of the classic German recipes that she would write about later in her cookbooks.

"The flavour of tomatoes with basil or melon with prosciutto," she says, "will forever remind me of my childhood summers spent with the Italian side of the family and the boisterous, happy meals at my aunt and uncle's table."

Luisa began collecting recipes when she was in college. She graduated and got a job as a book scout for publishers abroad. After a few years, she started her blog, *The Wednesday Chef*, and began to work through the mounds of recipes she had been stockpiling. Little did she know that her new hobby would change her life. She scored a job as a cookbook editor, leaned into her love of food, and soon her blog took off.

In 2010, she returned to Berlin with her husband and began to write full time. Her books include *My Berlin Kitchen*, *Classic German Baking*, and *Classic German Cooking*.

Luisa's expert advice for chefs in training? "Don't be afraid of a sharp knife."

Vanillepudding mit Erdbeersoße

SERVES 4 TO 6

"Vanillepudding mit Erdbeersoße (the ß, or eszett, is pronounced like the "s" in "see") is a traditional German dessert, often served at school cafeterias for a lunchtime dessert or whipped up in advance for an afternoon snack. This version of the classic is a simple cornflour pudding made with milk, real vanilla, and an egg yolk to add extra-silky richness. (Save the egg white to add to your scrambled eggs.) You can serve this pudding plain, but I think it's most delicious when eaten with a fresh berry sauce that is tangy and bright against the smooth, cool pudding.

The sauce is best made with in-season strawberries, which are sweet and full-flavoured. I add a little sugar and splash of lemon juice for an extra kick of acidity. The strawberries are cooked for only a few minutes, enough for them to almost fully break down, and then they are pureed. Depending on how much sauce you serve with the pudding, you may have some left over. It is delicious stirred into plain yoghurt or poured over a scoop of vanilla ice cream." –Luisa Weiss

!! 1. For the pudding: Pour 425 ml of the milk in a medium saucepan. If using the vanilla pod, place it on a chopping board. Using the tip of a paring knife, cut a thin slit all the way down the length of the pod without going through the bean. Now turn the blade of the knife so the sharp edge is against the inside of one of the pod halves. Starting at the top of the half, gently pull the knife down the length of the pod, and the inky black seeds will come out in a paste. Scrape this paste into the milk in the saucepan. Repeat with the other half of the pod and add the paste to the milk. If using the vanilla bean paste instead, add to the milk here. (Don't discard the scraped pod – just submerge it in a container of granulated sugar to flavour it over time.)

2. In a small bowl, whisk the cornflour into the remaining 60 ml milk, then whisk in the egg yolk until completely smooth.

3. Place the saucepan with the milk on the hob over medium heat and add the 3 tablespoons sugar and salt. Heat, stirring occasionally with the whisk and taking care not to let the milk boil.

Ingredients

Pudding

425 ml plus 60 ml whole milk, measured separately

1 vanilla pod, or 1 teaspoon vanilla bean paste

3 tablespoons cornflour

1 large egg yolk (see page 37)

3 tablespoons granulated sugar

¼ teaspoon table salt

Strawberry Sauce

340 g fresh strawberries, hulled and cut into quarters (see page 125)

Juice of ½ lemon (see page 12)

2 tablespoons granulated sugar

CONTINUED

If Luisa threw the Rebel dinner party of her dreams, she would invite Hildegard von Bingen, a medieval German mystic; Princess Diana; and Artemisia Gentileschi, an Italian Baroque painter. "I think the three of them would blow each other's minds," she says, "and I'd just be there to listen."

Vanillepudding mit Erdbeersoße
continued

4. After 4 to 6 minutes, small bubbles will begin to appear along the edges of the pan. Very slowly pour the cornflour mixture into the hot milk mixture while whisking constantly. Once all of the cornflour mixture is incorporated, turn off the stovetop and slide the saucepan to a cool burner. Continue to whisk until the whisk leaves traces in the pudding, about 30 seconds.

5. Use a rubber spatula to scrape the pudding into a serving bowl or four individual serving cups. Place cling film directly against the surface of the pudding to prevent a skin from forming. Let cool to room temperature, then transfer to the fridge for a few hours until well chilled.

6. **While the pudding chills, make the strawberry sauce:** Add the strawberries, lemon juice, and 2 tablespoons sugar to a small saucepan with a lid and use a silicone spatula to mix well.

7. Cover the pan with its lid and set over medium-high heat. As soon as the mixture starts to bubble, remove the lid and stir with the spatula. Lower the heat to medium-low and let the strawberries bubble away until almost completely broken down, 4 to 5 minutes.

8. Turn off the hob and carefully slide the saucepan to a cool part of the hob. Let cool for 5 to 10 minutes. Using an immersion blender, puree the strawberries in the pan until nearly smooth, leaving a few chunks for texture. Alternatively, you can carefully pour the mixture into a blender or food processor and blend to your desired consistency.

9. Let the sauce cool to room temperature, then transfer to an airtight container and chill in the fridge until ready to serve. The strawberry sauce will keep, in the fridge, for about 5 days.

10. If using individual cups, remove the cling film and use a spoon to top each portion with a few spoonfuls of sauce before serving. If using one serving bowl, put the sauce into a separate bowl and place alongside the pudding.

> A trip to Mexico changed Luisa's mind about coriander. Some home cooks served her tacos and guacamole. She says, "The skies parted, and I finally understood coriander! Now I love it."

PASTRIES, PUDDINGS, AND PIES

MAKES ONE 23 CM (9 IN) TART SHELL

SOUR CREAM PASTRY

Sour cream works wonders in pastry dough. It has enough moisture to hydrate the flour, plus additional fat that makes the dough extra tender and flaky. It's important to let the dough rest for at least 2 hours in the fridge after you make it – or, even better, overnight. As the dough rests, the flour will finish hydrating, the gluten in the flour will relax, and the little bits of butter will firm up, all of which will create flaky layers of pastry in a hot oven. If you're planning ahead, the dough can be made and stored in the fridge for up to 3 days before you use it.

INGREDIENTS

- 155 g plain flour
- 1 teaspoon granulated sugar
- ½ teaspoon table salt
- 120 g unsalted butter, cut into 1 cm (½ in) cubes and chilled
- 125 g sour cream

1. Add the flour, sugar, and salt to a **food processor** and lock the lid into place. Pulse until mixed, about three 1-second pulses.

2. Remove the processor lid and add the chilled butter cubes. Lock the lid back into place and pulse until the butter has broken down into coarse crumbs, eight to ten 1-second pulses.

3. Remove the processor lid and add the sour cream. Lock the lid back into place and process until the dough clumps together into tiny balls and no dry flour remains, 10 to 15 seconds.

4. Lay a piece of **cling film** on a worktop. Carefully remove the food processor blade. Use a **rubber spatula** to scrape the dough into the middle of the cling film (it will look crumbly, but that's OK!).

5. Gather and twist the edges of the cling film together towards the centre to form a tight bundle of dough. With the cling film still covering the dough, press the dough together to form it into a ball.

6. With the wrapped dough still on the worktop, use a **rolling pin** to flatten it into a disk 15 cm (6 in) in diameter, pushing the dough to the edges of the cling film. Use your fingers to press and rub together any cracks. Transfer the tightly wrapped dough to the fridge and chill for at least 2 hours or (even better!) up to overnight.

7. When ready to use, remove the chilled dough from the fridge and let it warm up on the worktop for 5 to 10 minutes. Follow the photos on the opposite page to roll out the dough. Use as directed in your recipe.

In her poem "The Electric Slide Boogie", poet Audre Lorde writes about how hard it is to sleep in the early hours of a New Year's Day morning. One of the many things she notices is "the edged aroma of slightly overdone Dutch apple pie".

REBEL GIRLS MAKE DESSERT

HOW TO ROLL OUT DOUGH

1

Lightly sprinkle a clean worktop with plain flour. Unwrap the dough, place it on the floured worktop, and sprinkle it with a little more flour.

2

Use a **rolling pin** to roll out the dough, working from the centre outwards to the top edge. Some recipes might call for using parchment paper on top of the dough before rolling it out. Rotate the dough a quarter turn clockwise and roll again from the centre to the top edge.

3

Keep rotating and rolling, sprinkling the worktop under the dough and the rolling pin with more flour as needed to prevent sticking, until the dough is an even 30 to 36 cm (12 to 14 in) circle (use the size specified in your recipe).

SERVES 8 TO 10

DUTCH APPLE PIE

INGREDIENTS

1 recipe Sour Cream Pastry (page 152), or one 30 cm (12 in) round shop-bought pie shell

3 large Granny Smith apples (about 680 g), peeled, cored, and sliced (see page 156)

3 large Gala, Pink Lady, or Honeycrisp apples (about 680 g), peeled, cored, and sliced (see page 156)

Juice of ½ small lemon (see page 12)

65 g brown sugar

55 g granulated sugar

3 tablespoons cornflour

2 teaspoons apple or pumpkin pie spice

¼ teaspoon table salt

1 recipe Crumble (page 116)

Using a combination of tart and sweet apples that keep their shape during baking is the secret to a great apple pie filling. Also essential? Letting the pie cool fully before slicing it! It can be hard to wait, but if you don't, the apple filling will be more soup than slice.

1. If using homemade dough, roll out the dough into a 33 cm (13 in) (see page 153) about 2.5–5 mm (⅛ to ¼ in) thick. Shape the dough into a pie shell (see page 157). Transfer the pie shell to the fridge until ready to use.

2. In a **large bowl**, use a **rubber spatula** to stir together all of the sliced apples and the lemon juice. Add the brown sugar, granulated sugar, cornflour, pie spice, and salt and stir until the apples are evenly coated. Let sit until the apples have released some of their juices, about 15 minutes.

3. Meanwhile, set an oven rack in the lower-middle position and heat the oven to 200°C. Line a **baking tray** with **aluminium foil**. Make the Crumble.

4. When the apples are ready, remove the pie shell from the fridge. Use your hands to arrange the apple slices inside the pie shell, layering them tightly so there are no gaps.

5. Use the rubber spatula to scrape any juices remaining in the bowl over the apples. Use your hands to pinch and sprinkle the Crumble evenly over the top of the apples.

6. Place the assembled pie on the foil-lined baking tray. Place the baking tray in the oven. Bake the pie until the crumble is golden brown, 35 to 40 minutes.

‼ 7. Use **oven gloves** to remove the baking tray from the oven and place it on the hob. Drape a large piece of **aluminium foil** over the pie so it is loosely covered (this creates a shield from the heat so the topping and crust won't burn while the filling continues to cook). Return the baking tray to the oven and continue to bake until the pie filling is bubbling and the crust and crumble are deep golden brown, about 30 minutes.

‼ 8. Use **oven gloves** to remove the baking tray from the oven and place it on the hob or a **cooling rack**. Let the pie cool for at least 4 hours or up to overnight. Slice and serve.

🔊 FUN FOOD FACT

According to legend, Granny Smith apples first appeared on the banks of a creek in a town just north of Sydney, Australia, in the 1860s. A woman named Maria Ann "Granny" Smith had been cooking with crab apples. She chucked the leftover apple cores into a heap outside, and soon an apple tree, with beautiful green fruits, sprouted.

HOW TO PEEL, CORE, AND CUT APPLES

1

Stand the apple, stem facing up, on a **chopping board**. Hold down the apple with your nondominant hand. With a **vegetable peeler** in your dominant hand, peel off one strip by starting at the top by the stem and moving downwards along the curve of the apple until you reach the bottom. Repeat until the whole apple is peeled.

!! 2

Use a **chef's knife** to slice around the apple core (where the stem is) to create four large pieces. Discard the core.

!! 3

Place each piece, flat side down, on the chopping board and cut it into 5 mm (¼ in) thick slices. Repeat these steps if you have more apples to cut.

HOW TO SHAPE A PIE SHELL

 **1**

Loosely roll the dough around the **rolling pin**. Unroll it over a **23 cm (9 in) pie dish**, letting the extra dough hang over the edges.

2

Working your way all the way around in a circle, gently fit the dough into the pie dish, lifting the edges as you press the bottom and sides flush against the dish. Use **kitchen scissors** to trim the edges of the dough to about 1 cm (½ in) beyond the edge of the pie dish.

3

Roll the 1 cm (½ in) overhang under itself so it sits on the rim of the pie dish. Pinch the dough, going all the way around the circle, so the edge stands up in a straight wall along the rim.

 4

To make a classic crimped crust, gently push a fold of dough out towards the edge of the dish with the thumb of one hand, and pinch the fold between the thumb and index finger of your other hand.

SERVES 4

RASPBERRY FOOL

This dessert takes its name from the French word *fouler* (pronounced "foo-lay"), which means "to press" or "to crush". Despite the French connection, a fool is a popular British dessert in which crushed or stewed fruits are swirled into whipped cream. Gooseberry and rhubarb are two favoured fruits to use in a fool in Britain, but raspberry fool was Queen Elizabeth II's favourite! If you're using frozen raspberries, there's no need to thaw them before adding them to the saucepan in step 1.

INGREDIENTS

275 g fresh or frozen raspberries, plus more fresh raspberries for decorating (optional)

55 g granulated sugar

Juice of ½ lemon (see page 12)

Pinch of table salt

1 recipe Whipped Cream (page 17)

1. In a **large saucepan**, combine the raspberries, sugar, lemon juice, and salt.

2. Place the saucepan on the hob over medium heat. Bring the mixture to a simmer (small bubbles appear all over the surface), then turn down the heat to medium-low and cook, stirring often with a **silicone spatula**, until the sugar has dissolved and the raspberries have softened and broken down, 7 to 9 minutes.

3. Turn off the hob and slide the saucepan to a cool part of the hob. Let cool slightly, about 5 minutes.

4. Use the spatula to scrape the raspberry mixture into a **large bowl** (be careful, as the saucepan and fruit mixture will still be warm). Let the raspberry mixture cool completely, at least 1 hour. After it's cool, you can cover and chill the mixture for up to 24 hours before continuing.

5. When you're ready to assemble your fool, whip the cream to soft peaks. Add about one-third of the whipped cream to the bowl with the cooled raspberry mixture. Using the silicone spatula, gently stir together until well mixed. Add the remaining whipped cream on top. Using the spatula, cut downwards through the mixture to the bottom of the bowl, then scrape along the bottom and up the side closest to you, scooping the mixture from the bottom and folding it over the top. Rotate the bowl a quarter turn and repeat, cutting downwards, scraping along the bottom and up the side, and folding over the top. Continue until the mixture is just combined but the whipped cream is still fluffy.

6. Divide the raspberry-cream mixture evenly among **small serving bowls** or **glasses**. Top the fool with fresh raspberries, if you like. Serve.

Queen Elizabeth II spent her summers at Balmoral Castle in Aberdeenshire, Scotland. Sometimes she and her sister, Princess Margaret, would pick berries from the garden and ask the chef to whip up desserts with them. One of her favourites was framboises St. George, which is raspberry fool topped with raspberries in the shape of a cross outlined with whipped cream. Yum!

RHUBARB FOOL

Use 225 g fresh or frozen sliced rhubarb in place of the raspberries. Increase the sugar to 75 g. In step 2, increase the cooking time to 8 to 10 minutes.

MEET CHEF ABI BALINGIT

In Abi's earliest kitchen memory, she is helping her mum stir a Filipino coconut and corn pudding called maja blanca. Abi always volunteered to lick the spoon! Her childhood sweet tooth hasn't dulled. It still helps to guide her as she makes her own spin on Filipino American food.

At 13, she began baking. Watching videos and reading online recipes, she threw herself into her new hobby. After attending college in California, Abi moved to New York City, where she rekindled her love of cooking. She would return home from work as the sun was going down and begin whipping up her creations, like passion fruit bars topped with Pop Rocks (popping candy) or lychee madeleines with hibiscus tea glaze and dried rose petals. Then she would share them on her blog, *The Dusky Kitchen*.

During the pandemic, she began making and selling pasalubong treat boxes to raise money for community-aid organizations. Pasalubong boxes are little treats Filipinos often buy for one another when they travel. A few thousand desserts later, and she had proved to herself that she could do amazing things in her tiny apartment kitchen.

In 2023, Abi published her first cookbook, *Mayumu: Filipino American Desserts Remixed*. For her, it is a dream come true. She says, "There's no better feeling than seeing people enjoy my recipes with their loved ones all over the world."

MANGO CREAM PIE

SERVES 8

"Growing up, I loved eating Sunflower Crackers Mango Cream Sandwiches for an after-school snack. This no-bake pie, with its cracker crust and creamy mango filling, is inspired by that favourite childhood snack in my Filipino household. The chilled pie is topped with juicy pearls of mango popping boba and a fluffy ribbon of whipped cream. If you'd rather serve the pie with canned whipped topping, feel free! Just note that it will dissolve faster than the homemade version. You can find Sunflower Crackers Mango Cream Sandwiches at a Filipino grocery shop or online. If you can't find the exact brand, you can use about 500 g Golden Oreos or other brand of vanilla sandwich cookies. I like to use a tin of mango juice for this recipe. Mango popping boba can be found at Asian supermarkets or online. Alternatively, you can dice up fresh mango to use for the topping." —Abi Balingit

INGREDIENTS

Crust

190 g package Sunflower Crackers Mango Cream Sandwiches (14 total sandwiches) or 500 g Golden Oreos

60 g unsalted butter, melted and cooled (see page 11)

Filling

60 ml water

7 g sachet unflavoured gelatin powder

250 ml mango juice

400 g tin sweetened condensed milk

½ teaspoon kosher salt

Topping

½ recipe Whipped Cream (page 17), or canned whipped cream

180 g mango popping boba, drained

1. **For the crust:** Add the cracker sandwiches (including the mango cream filling) to a *food processor* and lock the lid into place. Process until the sandwiches are reduced to fine crumbs, 15 to 30 seconds. Stop the processor.

2. Remove the processor lid and carefully remove the processor blade. Use a *rubber spatula* to transfer the cracker crumbs to a *large bowl*. Add the melted butter and mix with the spatula until well blended.

3. Dump the crumb-butter mixture into a *23 cm (9 in) pie dish* (regular, not deep dish!). Using the bottom of a *dry mug or glass*, press the crumb-butter mixture evenly onto the bottom and up the sides of the pan. You'll have to go around a few times to get the crumbs firmly and evenly shaped. Place the pie dish in the freezer to chill while you make the filling.

4. **For the filling:** Pour the water into a *measuring jug*. Sprinkle the gelatin powder evenly over the surface of the water. Set aside to bloom for 5 minutes, or until the mixture is the consistency of jelly.

PASTRIES, PUDDINGS, AND PIES

MANGO CREAM PIE
CONTINUED

5 While the gelatin is blooming, pour the mango juice into a **small saucepan** and bring to a boil over medium-high heat. Once the juice is boiling, turn off the hob and carefully pour the hot juice over the bloomed gelatin. Using a **whisk**, quickly stir until the gelatin has dissolved.

6 Add the sweetened condensed milk and salt to the gelatin mixture and whisk until well blended. Remove the pie dish from the freezer and pour the filling into the crust. Carefully place the pie uncovered in the fridge until the filling is well chilled and set, at least 3 hours or up to overnight.

7 **For the topping:** If you're making the whipped cream, whip the cream to stiff peaks. Fit a **piping bag** with a **large petal tip** (Ateco or Wilton #127) and fill the bag with the whipped cream. Pipe a ribbon border around the edge of the pie: with the wide part of the tip facing down closest to the surface of the pie, pipe in a back-and-forth motion while rotating the pie until you make a complete circle.

8 Decorate the centre of the pie with the mango popping boba. Serve and enjoy the pie cold. Store any leftover pie in an **airtight container** in the fridge for up to 3 days.

If Abi hosted any woman from history for dinner, she would choose Filipina food scientist and World War II hero María Orosa. María pioneered ways to use crops native to the Philippines. She invented banana ketchup and developed nutrient-rich darak, a rice by-product that was used to make cookies that saved soldiers' lives during the war. Abi would make Filipino spaghetti — with banana ketchup, of course!

CAPIROTADA DE AGUA

SERVES 6 TO 8

Capirotada is a bread pudding dessert traditionally served in Mexico during Lent and Easter. It's a sweet-salty mix of toasted bread, fruit, nuts, and melty cheese, all soaked in a spiced syrup-like mixture. It is often made with bolillos, Mexican bread rolls that have a crisp exterior and a pillowy interior. If you can't find bolillos near you, half a loaf of similarly light and fluffy supermarket French bread (usually found in the bakery section at the supermarket) works as well. Piloncillo, also called panela or panocha, is a type of raw cane sugar that's often used in Mexican and Latin American cooking and is typically sold in 115 g disks and 225 g cones. It has a warm, molasses-like flavour similar to brown sugar. If you can't find a 115 g disk, you can ask a grown-up for help breaking an 225 g cone in half (you'll need a sharp serrated knife to break up the hard sugar).

INGREDIENTS

- 2 to 3 bolillo rolls or ½ loaf French bread, cut into 2.5 cm (1 in) cubes
- 600 ml water
- 115 g piloncillo, or 130 g packed dark brown sugar
- 2 cinnamon sticks
- 2 whole cloves
- 1 banana
- Vegetable oil spray
- 60 g raisins
- 40 g salted roasted peanuts (optional)
- 115 g grated Oaxaca, Monterey Jack, or mozzarella cheese
- 1 tablespoon rainbow sprinkles (optional)

1. Set an oven rack in the middle position and heat the oven to 180°C.

2. Spread the bread cubes into an even layer on a **baking tray**. Place the baking tray in the oven. Bake until the bread is dried out and crispy when quickly tapped, 5 to 8 minutes.

⚠ 3. Use **oven gloves** to remove the baking tray from the oven and place it on the hob or a **cooling rack**. Let the bread cubes cool to room temperature, about 10 minutes.

4. Meanwhile, in a **large saucepan**, combine the water, piloncillo, cinnamon sticks, and cloves. Place the saucepan on the hob over medium heat. Bring the mixture to a simmer (small bubbles appear all over the surface), then lower the heat to medium-low and cook, stirring occasionally with a **silicone spatula**, until the sugar has dissolved and the mixture is fragrant, about 10 minutes. Turn off the hob and slide the saucepan to a cool part of the hob. Let cool slightly, about 5 minutes.

5. While the piloncillo mixture cools, peel the banana, place it on a **chopping board**, and use a **butter knife** to cut it into 5 mm (¼ in) thick rounds.

6. Spray an **20 cm (8 in) square** or other **2 litre glass** or **ceramic baking dish** with vegetable oil spray. Add half of the cooled bread cubes to the greased baking dish. Top the bread cubes

CONTINUED

PASTRIES, PUDDINGS, AND PIES

CAPIROTADA DE AGUA
CONTINUED

evenly with all of the banana slices, half of the raisins, and half of the peanuts (if using). Then sprinkle with half of the cheese. Repeat the layering with the remaining bread cubes, raisins, peanuts (if using), and cheese.

7 Use a **spoon** to remove and discard the cinnamon sticks and cloves from the warm piloncillo mixture. Carefully transfer the warm mixture to a **measuring jug** or **medium bowl with a spout**. Pour the mixture over the bread mixture in the baking dish, making sure to soak all of the bread evenly.

8 Place the baking dish in the oven. Bake until the pudding is bubbling and the cheese is golden brown, 40 to 45 minutes.

!! 9 Use **oven gloves** to remove the baking dish from the oven and place it on the hob or a **cooling rack**. Scatter the sprinkles (if using) evenly over the top. Let the capirotada cool for at least 10 minutes. Serve warm.

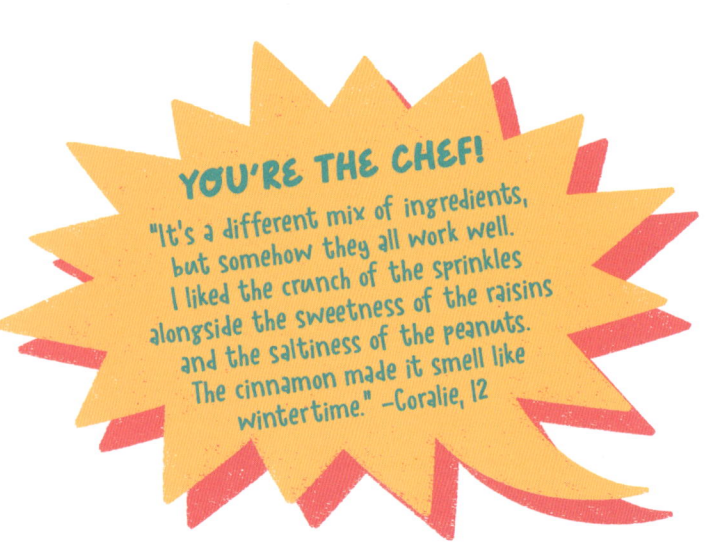

YOU'RE THE CHEF!
"It's a different mix of ingredients, but somehow they all work well. I liked the crunch of the sprinkles alongside the sweetness of the raisins and the saltiness of the peanuts. The cinnamon made it smell like wintertime." —Coralie, 12

BANANA PUDDING

SERVES 6 TO 8

This style of banana pudding isn't banana-flavoured pudding at all. It is a dessert consisting of layers of sweet Nilla Wafers, sliced bananas, and creamy vanilla pudding. It's a beloved recipe in the American South that is taken to many large gatherings. Assembling this pudding in a 22 by 12 cm (8½ by 4½ inch) clear glass loaf tin or other clear 1.5 litre container shows off its fun layers, but you can use any nontransparent serving dish of your choice instead. It will taste just as delicious!

INGREDIENTS

- 165 g granulated sugar
- 30 g cornflour
- Pinch of table salt
- 2 large whole eggs plus 2 large egg yolks (see page 37)
- 750 ml whole milk
- 30 g unsalted butter, cut into 1-tablespoon pieces and chilled
- 1 teaspoon vanilla extract
- 3 ripe bananas
- Juice of ½ small lemon (see page 12)
- 85 g Nilla Wafer cookies, or 85 g vanilla wafers, plus more for decorating
- 1 recipe Whipped Cream (page 17), or canned whipped cream

1. Set a **fine-mesh sieve** over a **large heatproof bowl** and place it next to the hob. In a **large saucepan**, **whisk** together the sugar, cornflour, and salt. Whisk in the whole eggs and egg yolks until blended, then whisk in the milk until everything is evenly combined.

2. Place the saucepan over medium heat and cook the mixture, using a **silicone spatula** to stir constantly and to scrape the bottom and sides of the saucepan, until the mixture begins to thicken and bubble, 7 to 10 minutes. (Once the pudding begins to thicken and bubble, be careful not to cook it any longer, as too much heat can cause the eggs to scramble.)

‼3. Turn off the hob and slide the saucepan to a cool part of the hob. Using the spatula, immediately scrape the pudding into the fine-mesh sieve and stir and push it through the sieve into the bowl (be careful, as the saucepan and pudding will be hot). Discard any solids left behind in the sieve.

4. **Whisk** the chilled butter and vanilla into the pudding until melted and evenly mixed. Let the pudding cool slightly, at least 10 minutes or up to 30 minutes.

5. Meanwhile, peel the bananas and place them on a **chopping board**. Use a **butter knife** to slice them into 5 mm (¼ in) thick rounds. Place the banana slices in a **medium bowl** and drizzle the lemon juice over them. Use a **spoon** to stir until the bananas are evenly coated (this helps to keep them from turning brown).

CONTINUED

PASTRIES, PUDDINGS, AND PIES

BANANA PUDDING
CONTINUED

📢 FUN FOOD FACT

Magnolia Bakery in New York City is famous for its classic banana pudding. Since the banana dessert took off, Bobbie Lloyd, the CEO and chief baking officer at Magnolia, has experimented with other banana pudding recipes, including rainbow, s'mores, red velvet, and salted caramel.

6 Add enough cookies to a **1.5 litre clear glass loaf tin**, **bowl**, or **other clear container** to cover the bottom (the cookies can overlap as needed). Arrange half of the banana slices in a layer over the cookies, covering the cookies completely. Spoon half of the cooled vanilla pudding on top of the banana slices and spread into an even layer with the back of the spoon. Repeat the layering with the remaining cookies, banana slices, and pudding.

7 Gently press a sheet of **cling film** onto the surface of the pudding (this helps prevent a skin from forming on top). Transfer to the fridge and chill for at least 1 hour and up to 2 days (the cookies will get softer the longer the pudding chills).

8 If you're making the whipped cream, just before you're ready to serve, whip the cream to soft peaks. Top the pudding with the whipped cream and decorate with more crushed or whole cookies as desired. Serve.

SERVES 12 TO 16

CHOCOFLAN

INGREDIENTS

Cake
Vegetable oil spray
165 g plain flour
200 g granulated sugar
50 g unsweetened Dutch-processed or natural cocoa powder
¾ teaspoon baking powder
¾ teaspoon bicarbonate of soda
½ teaspoon table salt
250 ml whole milk
120 ml vegetable oil
1 large egg
120 ml cajeta or caramel dessert sauce

Flan
400 g tin sweetened condensed milk
350 g tin evaporated milk
115 g full-fat cream cheese, cut into 2.5 cm (1 in) pieces and softened (see page 11)
1 tablespoon vanilla extract
3 large eggs

Chocoflan is a popular dessert in Mexico that's also known as pastel imposible, or "impossible cake". What's seemingly impossible about it is that it does a magic trick in the oven: the cake layer starts out on the bottom of the pan with the flan on top, but they swap places as they bake! You can find cajeta in Latin American shops or online. If you can't find it, you can use a caramel dessert sauce (like the kind you'd drizzle on an ice cream sundae), but don't substitute it with dulce de leche, which is too thick for this recipe. Plan ahead. This dessert needs to chill overnight in the fridge after baking for the flan layer to firm up.

1. **For the cake layer:** Set an oven rack in the middle position and heat the oven to 180°C. Spray the inside of a **26 cm (10 in) Bundt** or **ring tin** generously with vegetable oil spray. Place the Bundt tin inside a **large roasting tin** with sides at least 5 cm (2 in) tall.

2. In a **medium bowl**, **whisk** together the flour, sugar, cocoa powder, baking powder, bicarbonate of soda, and salt.

3. In a **large bowl**, whisk together the milk, oil, and 1 egg until well blended.

4. Add the flour mixture to the milk mixture and stir with a **rubber spatula** until just combined and no dry flour remains (make sure to scrape along the bottom and sides of the bowl). Set aside.

5. Add the cajeta to a **small microwave-safe bowl**. Microwave at 100 per cent power until pourable but not hot, 10 to 30 seconds. Pour the cajeta into the greased Bundt tin.

6. Use a **pastry brush** to paint the cajeta up the sides of the tin all the way around. (It will slide back down a bit, but that's OK.) Scrape the cake batter into the Bundt tin on top of the cajeta, pouring it in an even layer.

7. **For the flan layer:** Add the sweetened condensed milk, evaporated milk, softened cream cheese, vanilla, and 3 eggs to a **blender**. Put the lid on the blender and hold it in place with a **folded kitchen towel**. Blend on medium-high speed until smooth, about 30 seconds.

8. Slowly and gently pour the flan mixture into the Bundt tin, trying to keep it on top of the cake batter without swirling

YOU'RE THE CHEF!
"The cake was moist and had a nice rich chocolate flavour. The flan's texture reminded me of pudding, and it goes well with the chocolate cake. Very fun to make!"
—Olivia, 14

CHOCOFLAN
CONTINUED

in too much. Cut a piece of **aluminium foil** large enough to cover the top of the Bundt tin and spray one side with vegetable oil spray. Cover the top of the tin with the foil, greased side down, and seal and crimp the edges.

⚠ 9 Bring a **kettle** of water to a boil. Pour the water into the roasting tin to reach 2.5–5 cm (1–2 in) up the sides of the Bundt tin.

⚠ 10 Ask a grown-up to carefully transfer the roasting tin to the oven (the pan will be heavy and hot). Bake until the top of the cake has puffed to the top of the tin and a toothpick inserted into the cake layer comes out clean (carefully peel back the foil to check), about 1 hour and 15 minutes.

⚠ 11 Use **oven gloves** to remove the Bundt tin from the water in the roasting tin and place it on the hob or a **cooling rack**. (Be careful, as the water and the roasting pan will be very hot! You can let the roasting tin and its water cool in the turned-off oven before emptying and cleaning the tin.) Carefully peel the foil from the top of the Bundt tin and reserve for later.

12 Let the chocoflan cool until just warm, about 1½ hours. Re-cover with the foil and transfer the warm chocoflan to the fridge. Chill until set, at least 8 hours or up to 24 hours.

13 When ready to serve, remove the Bundt tin from the fridge and remove the foil. Use a **butter knife** to loosen the edges of the cake from the sides and middle of the tin.

14 Fill a **large bowl** halfway with hot tap water. Hold the bottom third of the Bundt tin in the hot water for 1 minute to loosen up the cajeta. Remove the Bundt tin from the water.

⚠ 15 Turn a **large, flat platter** upside down on top of the Bundt tin. Holding the platter and cake tin together firmly, flip them over and place the platter on the worktop. Jiggle the platter back and forth gently a few times until you see or hear the chocoflan release from the tin. Lift the Bundt tin off the chocoflan, letting the cajeta drizzle down the sides. Use a **spoon** to scrape any leftover cajeta from the bottom of the tin and drizzle it over the top of the flan. Slice and serve.

CHERRY GALETTE

SERVES 4 TO 6

A galette is a simpler take on a fruit tart. A flaky pastry crust is still involved, but instead of shaping it in a tart tin or pie dish, you fold up the edges and bake the galette flat on a baking tray. It's great if you like your dessert with more crust than filling. The demerara sugar creates a sparkly, crunchy crust, but granulated sugar can be used in a pinch. The galette is yummy as is, but we love to add a scoop of vanilla ice cream to make this à la mode.

INGREDIENTS

1 recipe Sour Cream Pastry (page 152), or one 30 cm (12 in) round shop-bought pastry shell

340 g frozen sweet cherries, thawed (see intro paragraph on page 123)

1 tablespoon cornflour

¼ teaspoon vanilla extract

Pinch of table salt

1 large egg

1 teaspoon demerara sugar

1. Set an oven rack in the middle position and heat the oven to 190°C. Line a **baking tray** with **parchment paper**.

2. If using homemade dough, roll out the dough into a 30 cm (12 in) circle about 5 mm (¼ in) thick (see page 153). Transfer the dough circle to the parchment-lined baking tray. Place the baking tray in the fridge and let the dough chill for 10 to 15 minutes.

3. While the dough chills, in a **large bowl**, combine the thawed cherries, cornflour, vanilla, and salt. Use a **rubber spatula** to stir until the cherries are well coated.

4. Remove the baking tray from the fridge. Use a **large spoon** to transfer the cherry mixture to the centre of the dough circle, spreading the mixture out and leaving a 5 cm (2 in) border around the edges.

5. Fold the dough over the edge of the filling, slightly overlapping the dough every 5 cm (2 in) and working all the way around the circle.

6. Crack the egg into a **small bowl**. Beat lightly with a **fork** until blended. Use a **pastry brush** to paint the edges of the dough with the beaten egg. Sprinkle the crust evenly with the sugar.

7. Place the baking tray in the oven. Bake until the crust is golden brown, 25 to 30 minutes.

⚠ 8. Use **oven gloves** to remove the baking tray from the oven and place it on the hob or a **cooling rack**. Let the galette cool on the baking try for at least 15 minutes.

CONTINUED

PASTRIES, PUDDINGS, AND PIES

CHERRY GALETTE
CONTINUED

!! 9 Use a **wide spatula** to transfer the galette to a **chopping board**. Use a **chef's knife** to cut into wedges. Serve warm.

CHERRY CHOCOLATE GALETTE

In step 3, add 90 g dark chocolate chips to the large bowl with the thawed cherries, cornflour, vanilla, and salt.

📢 FUN FOOD FACT

In 2007, singer-songwriter Lisa Loeb released a song called "Life Is Just a Bowl of Cherries". In it, she reminds listeners to live, laugh, love, and not take life too seriously. You can't take your money with you when you go, she wrote, "So keep repeating: 'It's the berries'".

YOU'RE THE CHEF!
"It was so very easy to make, it looked beautiful, and it tasted delicious!" –Hannah, 8

LEMON POSSETS

SERVES 6

INGREDIENTS
2 to 3 lemons
500 ml double cream
150 g granulated sugar

A posset is a traditional British dessert that dates back to the 17th century. It uses the power of acidic fruit juice to thicken cream into a spoonable, creamy, pudding-like treat. This version features lemon (the most classic flavour for posset), using both lemon juice and strips of flavourful zest. For an extra-special presentation, serve these possets topped with fresh berries or a drizzle of Strawberry Sauce (page 149).

1. Use a **vegetable peeler** to peel three long strips of zest from 1 lemon. Then juice the lemons (see page 12) to measure 75 ml juice.

2. In a **large saucepan**, combine the cream, sugar, and lemon zest strips. Stir with a **silicone spatula** until the sugar is mostly dissolved.

3. Place the pan over medium heat and bring the cream mixture to a boil. Cook, stirring often with the spatula (the mixture will bubble up quite a lot in the pan!) for 5 minutes. Turn off the hob and slide the saucepan to a cool part of the hob.

4. Stir in the lemon juice and let the mixture cool for 20 minutes.

5. Use **tongs** or a **spoon** to remove the lemon zest strips from the cream mixture and discard. Stir the mixture once with the spatula (it will have started to thicken up) and then transfer it to a **measuring jug** or **medium bowl with a spout**.

6. Pour the mixture into **six 115 g ramekins** or **small glasses**, dividing it evenly. Place in the fridge uncovered, until well chilled and firm, about 3 hours. Once the possets are set, they can be covered with **cling film** and fridge for up to 2 days. Serve.

FUN FOOD FACT

English author Elizabeth Moxon included five posset recipes in her 1789 book *English Housewifery*, including a lemon posset, an ale posset, a posset with almonds, and two different possets made with fortified wine. She suggested serving them up in glasses or china dishes. Today, home cooks share colourful social media photos of possets served in hollowed-out lemon halves.

176   REBEL GIRLS MAKE DESSERT

Guyanese Pine Tarts

MAKES 4 TARTS

These individual-size pastries are a signature sweet of Guyana, a small country on the northeast coast of South America. The "pine" of the title is short for the sweet, jam-like pineapple filling tucked inside the triangle-shaped crust. The tarts are traditionally made with fresh pineapple, but this recipe uses a tin of crushed pineapple for ease. For even more ease, you can split this project up over a couple of days. The cooled pineapple filling can be covered and chilled in the fridge for up to 2 days before using, and the cut-out dough circles can be chilled for up to 1 day.

You can use light brown sugar for a more delicate flavour, or dark brown sugar if you prefer deeper molasses notes. If using shop-bought tart shell, the package often comes with two dough rounds. Use just one for this recipe and save the other one for making a Dutch Apple Pie (page 154) or a Cherry Galette (page 173).

Ingredients

- 225 g tin crushed pineapple
- 65 g brown sugar
- ½ teaspoon vanilla extract
- ¼ teaspoon ground cinnamon
- Pinch of ground nutmeg
- Pinch of table salt
- 1 recipe Sour Cream Pastry (page 152), or one 30 cm (12 in) round shop-bought tart shell
- 1 large egg
- 1 tablespoon water

1. In a **25 cm (10 in) nonstick frying pan**, combine the pineapple (including the juice), brown sugar, vanilla, cinnamon, nutmeg, and salt.

2. Place the frying pan on the hob over medium heat. Bring the mixture to a simmer (small bubbles appear all over the surface), then lower the heat to medium-low and cook, stirring often with a **silicone spatula**, until the pineapple has softened, the liquid has evaporated, and the spatula leaves a clear trail when scraped across the bottom of the frying pan, 10 to 12 minutes.

3. Turn off the hob and slide the frying pan to a cool part of the hob. Let cool slightly, about 5 minutes.

4. Use the silicone spatula to scrape the pineapple mixture into a **shallow medium dish** (be careful, as the frying pan and the pineapple mixture will still be hot). Let cool to room temperature, about 30 minutes.

CONTINUED

PASTRIES, PUDDINGS, AND PIES

GUYANESE PINE TARTS
CONTINUED

5 While the pineapple mixture is cooling, line a **baking tray** with **parchment paper**. If using homemade dough, roll out the dough into a 33 cm (13 in) circle about 3 mm (⅛ in) thick (see page 153).

!! 6 Find a **bowl** or **round container lid** that is 15 cm (6 in) in diameter. Place the overturned bowl or lid on the dough and use a **paring knife** to trace around it to cut out three 15 cm (6 in) circles of dough. Transfer the dough circles to the parchment-lined baking tray.

7 Gather the dough scraps together into a ball and re-roll it into a circle of the same thickness and about 23 cm (9 in) in diameter. Cut out one more 15 cm (6 in) circle and add it to the baking tray (you'll have four circles in total). Discard the remaining dough scraps. Cover the dough circles with **cling film** and place the baking sheet in the fridge to chill for at least 10 minutes or until the pineapple filling is fully cooled.

8 When ready to assemble your tarts, set an oven rack in the middle position and heat the oven to 180°C. Crack the egg into a **small bowl** and add the water. Beat lightly with a **fork** until blended.

9 Remove the baking tray with the dough circles from the fridge. Fill and shape your pine tarts (see the photos on the opposite page). If the dough is very firm from chilling and cracks when folded, let it soften for 5 to 10 minutes on the worktop before continuing with shaping.

10 Place the baking tray in the oven. Bake the tarts until the crust is golden brown, 25 to 30 minutes.

!! 11 Use **oven gloves** to remove the baking tray from the oven and place it on the hob or a **cooling rack**. Let the tarts cool completely on the baking tray, about 30 minutes. Serve.

REBEL IN THE KITCHEN

As a kid in Guyana, Yonette Alleyne's mother never let her help in the kitchen. For her 11th birthday, Yonette asked for a chef's coat, hat, and gloves. She got them, along with a cookbook. Excited, she baked a batch of cupcakes . . . but she forgot to add the baking powder. Since then, she has perfected her cooking and now owns and operates the Caribbean Gourmet in the San Gabriel Valley in California.

HOW TO SHAPE PINE TARTS

Use a **1-tablespoon measuring spoon** to divide the pineapple filling evenly among the four dough circles, placing about 2 tablespoons in the centre of each circle. Spread the filling into a 7.5 cm (3 in) circle.

Working with one dough circle at a time, use a **pastry brush** to paint the edges of the circle with the beaten egg. Fold the bottom 4 cm (1½ in) of the circle towards the centre, letting it rest on the filling.

Fold the left side of the circle over on a diagonal, overlapping the bottom and gently pressing the dough together where the edges meet. Fold the right side of the circle over to form a triangle shape, overlapping the other two sides and covering all of the filling. Gently press the corners together.

Repeat steps 2 and 3 to shape the remaining tarts. Use the pastry brush to paint the tops of the tarts with more beaten egg.

SERVES 4

THIAKRY

Thiakry is a West African dessert especially common in Senegal and The Gambia. It's a creamy pudding traditionally made from millet, a gluten-free round grain widely cultivated in the area. Wheat couscous, which is made from semolina flour, is often another option for this pudding. If using millet for this recipe, make sure to follow the cooking instructions on the packet for step 1.

INGREDIENTS

300 ml water

185 g couscous or millet

120 ml sweetened condensed milk

125 g plain whole-milk Greek yoghurt

120 ml whole milk, plus more if needed

1 teaspoon vanilla extract

½ teaspoon ground cinnamon

¼ teaspoon ground nutmeg

Raisins and/or chopped nuts, for serving (optional)

1. In a **small saucepan**, bring the water to a boil over medium-high heat. Add the couscous and stir with a **silicone spatula**. Turn off the hob, slide the saucepan to a cool part of the hob, and cover the pan with a **lid**. Let sit until the water has been absorbed, about 5 minutes.

2. Meanwhile, in a **large bowl**, combine the sweetened condensed milk, yoghurt, milk, vanilla, cinnamon, and nutmeg. **Whisk** until well combined.

3. Use the spatula to transfer the couscous to the large bowl and then stir until well mixed, making sure to break up any clumps of couscous. Cover the bowl with **cling film** and chill in the fridge until chilled, about 30 minutes.

4. When the pudding is chilled, remove the cling film and stir the pudding with the spatula. If the pudding is too thick, add more milk, 1 tablespoon at a time, until it reaches the consistency you like.

5. Divide the pudding evenly among **four serving bowls** and top with raisins and/or nuts, if desired. Serve.

 REBEL IN THE KITCHEN

Mame Sow grew up in Dakar, Senegal. Now she is a pastry chef in New York City. She says, "For us, in Dakar, food is a celebration. It's a way for us to show love and welcome people." She grew up eating ice lollies made with tropical flowers and fruits, like hibiscus and baobab. Today, she calls on her Senegalese roots to create desserts that incorporate hibiscus, baobab, peanuts, cashews, vanilla, chocolate, and different spices. Her desserts are her "love letter to Africa".

GUAVA AND CHEESE PASTELITOS

MAKES 4 PASTELITOS

Pastelitos are classic Cuban pastries often enjoyed with a strong but sweet cup of café con leche. The combination of sweet guava paste and tangy cream cheese makes for a lovely treat any time of day. Guava paste is sold packaged in different shapes, but don't worry too much about the shape of the pieces you cut for the pastelitos. As long as each piece fits on half of each puff pastry square, you're golden! To thaw frozen puff pastry, let it sit in the refrigerator overnight, or unwrap it and let it sit on the worktop at room temperature until pliable but not too soft, about 30 minutes.

1. Set an oven rack in the middle position and heat the oven to 200°C. Line a **baking tray** with **parchment paper**.

2. In a **small bowl**, combine the cream cheese, vanilla, lemon zest (if using), and salt. Use a **spoon** to stir until well mixed.

!! 3. Unfold the puff pastry on a **chopping board**. Use a **bench scraper** or **chef's knife** to cut the pastry into four equal squares. Transfer the pastry squares to the parchment-lined baking tray.

!! 4. Place the guava paste on the chopping board and use the bench scraper or chef's knife to cut it into four equal pieces. Place one piece on the left half of each square. Place 1 tablespoon of the cream cheese mixture on top of each piece of guava paste.

5. Crack the egg into a **small bowl**. Beat lightly with a **fork** until blended. Use a **pastry brush** to paint the edges of each pastry square with the beaten egg.

6. Fold the empty right side of each pastry square over the filling and use your fingers to firmly press the edges together.

7. Paint the top and sides of each pastelito with the rest of the beaten egg. Sprinkle the pastries with the sugar, dividing it evenly.

8. Place the baking tray in the oven. Bake until the pastries are puffed and golden, 18 to 20 minutes.

!! 9. Use **oven gloves** to remove the baking tray from the oven and place it on the hob or a **cooling rack**. Let the pastelitos cool on the baking tray for at least 10 minutes. Serve warm.

INGREDIENTS

60 g full-fat cream cheese, cut into 2.5 cm (1 in) pieces and softened (see page 11)

½ teaspoon vanilla extract

¼ teaspoon grated lemon zest (optional; see page 12)

Pinch of table salt

1 (23 cm (9 in) square) sheet puff pastry, thawed

115 g guava paste

1 large egg

1 teaspoon demerara or granulated sugar

REBEL IN THE KITCHEN

In 1948, chef Nitza Villepol began hosting the TV cooking show *Cocina al Minuto* in Cuba. She started off cooking classic Cuban food, but her recipes changed with the times. After the Cuban Revolution, the island country was increasingly isolated, and many ingredients were hard to get. Resourceful and creative, she began to teach folks how to cook with what was available.

PASTRIES, PUDDINGS, AND PIES

SERVES 4

OAT MILK CHOCOLATE PUDDING

INGREDIENTS

110 g granulated sugar

40 g unsweetened Dutch-processed cocoa powder

3 tablespoons cornflour

½ teaspoon vanilla extract

Pinch of table salt

750 ml unsweetened oat milk

90 g vegan dark chocolate chips

This is a super-speedy pudding that's extra chocolatey. Oat milk is especially creamy, which makes it the best non-dairy milk choice here. If you have leftover pudding, it can be stored in the fridge for up to 3 days. Just make sure to press a piece of cling film directly onto the surface of the pudding before storing it to prevent a skin from forming.

1. In a **medium saucepan**, **whisk** together the sugar, cocoa powder, cornflour, vanilla, and salt.

2. Add the oat milk and whisk until well blended. Place the pan over medium-low heat and cook the mixture, whisking constantly, until it thickens, 5 to 7 minutes. Turn off the hob and slide the saucepan to a cool part of the hob.

3. Add the chocolate chips to the pudding and use a **rubber spatula** to stir until the chips have melted and the pudding is smooth and shiny, about 30 seconds. Carefully transfer the pudding to **four serving bowls** (the saucepan and pudding will be warm!). Serve warm.

REBEL IN THE KITCHEN

Pastry chef Talia Profet specializes in experimenting with cocoa powder. She says, "Most people think cocoa equals chocolate, but actually it's the other way around: chocolate derives from the cocoa bean." She has used cocoa powder with all kinds of flavours, including guava, miso, turmeric, smoked vanilla, and orange.

MANGO SAGO

SERVES 4 TO 6

INGREDIENTS

120 g plus 40 g diced fresh or frozen mango, thawed if frozen (see intro paragraph on page 123), measured separately

75 ml sweetened condensed milk

250 ml light unsweetened coconut milk

225 g small pearl tapioca

1.4 litres water

Sago pudding is a refreshing dessert found across many different cultures. The pudding has a fun chewy texture thanks to the addition of sago, or tapioca pearls. Make sure to use small tapioca pearls for this recipe, not quick tapioca or mini tapioca (and definitely not tapioca pearls made for bubble tea or boba). This recipe gets a lot of its sweetness from the mango. If your mango isn't very sweet, you can add extra sweetened condensed milk to the pudding before dividing it into serving bowls. Add 1 tablespoon at a time, stirring and tasting after each addition.

1. Add 120 g of the mango, the sweetened condensed milk, and coconut milk to a food processor and lock the lid into place. Process until smooth, about 1 minute. Stop the processor. (This step can also be done in a blender.)

!!2. Remove the lid and carefully remove the processor blade. Use a rubber spatula to transfer the mango mixture to a large bowl.

3. Set a large fine-mesh sieve by the sink. In a large saucepan, combine the tapioca pearls and water. Place the pan over medium-high heat and cook, stirring occasionally with a wooden spoon or silicone spatula, until the pearls become translucent, 5 to 7 minutes, or according to packet instructions. Turn off the hob. If you can still see a small white spot in the tapioca pearls after cooking, slide the pan to a cool part of the hob and cover with a lid for about 10 minutes.

!!4. Place the sieve in the sink and drain the cooked tapioca pearls into the sieve. Hold the pearls under cold running water until cooled down, about 1 minute. Transfer the cooled tapioca pearls to the large bowl with the mango mixture.

5. Use the spatula to gently stir together the tapioca pearls and mango mixture until well mixed. Divide the pudding evenly among four serving bowls. Top with the remaining 40 g diced mango, dividing it evenly. Serve.

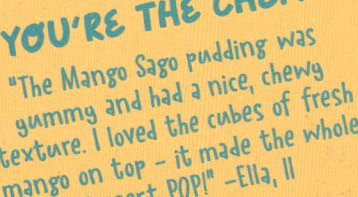

YOU'RE THE CHEF!
"The Mango Sago pudding was gummy and had a nice, chewy texture. I loved the cubes of fresh mango on top – it made the whole dessert POP!" –Ella, 11

CHOCOLATE TARTE SOLEIL
WITH DULCE DE LECHE DIPPING SAUCE

SERVES 6 TO 8

INGREDIENTS

90 g dark chocolate chips

1 tablespoon plus 2 tablespoons double cream, measured separately

Plain flour, for dusting

2 (23 cm (9 in) square) sheets frozen puff pastry, thawed

1 large egg

1 tablespoon demerara sugar (optional)

120 ml tinned dulce de leche

¼ teaspoon ground cinnamon

Pinch of table salt

A tarte soleil looks fancy but is secretly easy to make! It's shaped to look like a sun (the word *soleil* means "sun" in French). To thaw frozen puff pastry, let it sit in the fridge overnight, or unwrap it and let it sit on the worktop at room temperature until pliable but not too soft, about 30 minutes. If you can't find tinned dulce de leche, you can use jarred caramel dessert sauce instead. If you substitute the caramel sauce, reduce the cream to 1 tablespoon, as dulce de leche is much thicker.

1. Set an oven rack in the middle position and heat the oven to 190°C. Line a **baking tray** with **parchment paper**.

2. Place the chocolate chips and 1 tablespoon cream in a **small microwave-safe bowl**. Microwave at 50 per cent power until melted, 1 to 2 minutes, stopping the microwave and stirring with a **spoon** every 30 seconds.

3. Remove the bowl from the microwave and stir the mixture until completely melted and smooth. Set aside to cool until just warm, about 15 minutes.

4. Crack the egg into a **small bowl**. Beat lightly with a **fork** until blended.

5. Lightly sprinkle a clean worktop with flour. Unfold the first piece of puff pastry on the floured worktop. Use a **rolling pin** to gently roll the pastry into a 25 cm (10 in) square. Follow the photos on page 193 to assemble and shape your tarte soleil, placing the pastry on the lined baking tray. Use a **pastry brush** to paint the tart all over with the beaten egg. Sprinkle evenly with the sugar (if using).

6. Place the baking tray in the oven. Bake until the tart is puffed and deep golden brown, 25 to 30 minutes.

CONTINUED

PASTRIES, PUDDINGS, AND PIES

CHOCOLATE TARTE SOLEIL
WITH DULCE DE LECHE DIPPING SAUCE
CONTINUED

⚠️ 7. Use **oven gloves** to remove the baking tray from the oven and place it on the hob or a **cooling rack**. Let the tart cool on the baking tray for at least 10 minutes.

8. While the tart is cooling, combine the dulce de leche, cinnamon, salt, and the remaining 2 tablespoons cream in a **second small microwave-safe bowl**.

9. Microwave at 50 per cent power until the dulce de leche is warm and fluid, 1 to 2 minutes, stopping the microwave and stirring with a **clean spoon** every 30 seconds.

10. Remove the bowl from the microwave and stir the mixture until well blended and smooth. Transfer the warm sauce to the drinking glass you used when shaping the tart or to a **small serving bowl**.

11. Transfer the cooled tarte soleil to a **serving platter**. Place the glass or bowl of sauce in the centre of the tarte soleil and serve. Enjoy by tearing off sections of pastry and dipping them into the warm sauce.

 REBEL IN THE KITCHEN

Dulce de leche is made by cooking milk and sugar together until a thick, brown, sweet sauce forms. Mexican cajeta is similar but made from goat's milk. The first-known Spanish language recipes were recorded in the late 1600s by Sor Juana Inés de la Cruz, a Mexican nun and poet, who wrote a piece called "rules for all cajetas". Thirty-six of her recipes still exist today, and most are for sweets.

HOW TO SHAPE A TARTE SOLEIL

1

Place a 23 cm (9 in) cake tin (or an upside-down mixing bowl with a similar diameter) on the 25 cm (10 in) pastry square. Use a paring knife to trace around the tin and cut out a circle of pastry. Transfer the pastry circle to the parchment-lined baking sheet and discard the scraps. Repeat tracing and cutting to make a second circle from the second sheet of puff pastry, but don't put it on the baking tray yet.

2

Use a small offset spatula or spoon to spread the cooled chocolate mixture on the first pastry circle on the baking tray, leaving a 1 cm (½ in) border. Place the second pastry circle on top of the first and press down gently to stick the layers together.

3

Place a small drinking glass or jar upside down in the centre of the pastry circle. Starting from the edge of the glass and going outward, use the paring knife to cut the circle into quarters, cutting down through both layers of pastry (the centre will be intact under the glass). Use the paring knife to cut each quarter into four equal pieces, forming 16 sections total (like the rays of the sun!).

4

Holding the end of one of the sections, gently twist it three times into a spiral. Gently press the end of the section onto the parchment. Repeat twisting the remaining sections all the way around the tart. Remove the glass from the centre of the tart.

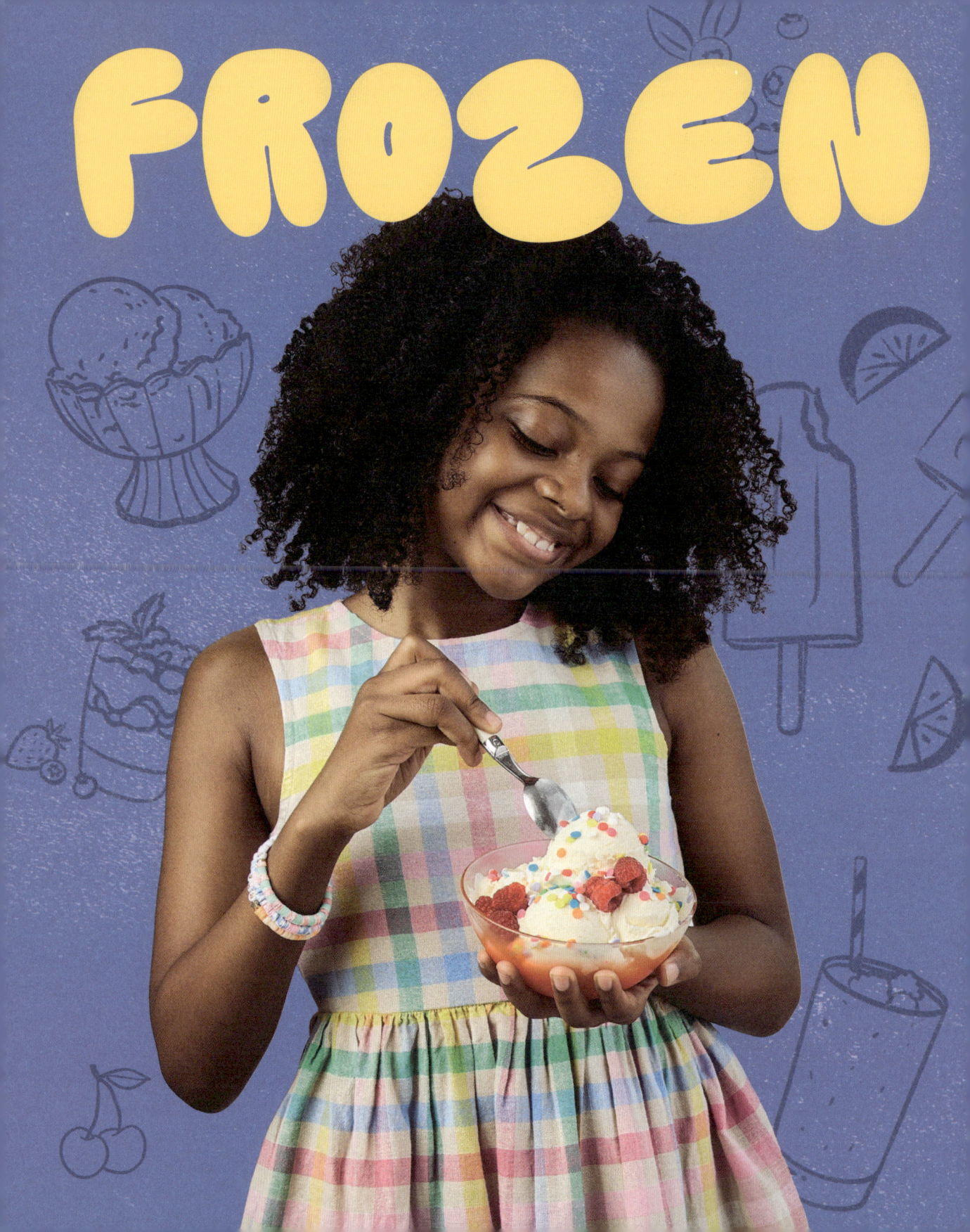

TREATS

197 Kiwi-Berry Frozen Lemonade Lollies
  Apricot-Berry Frozen Lemonade Lollies

198 Vanilla No-Churn Ice Cream
  Mint Chocolate Chip No-Churn Ice Cream

199 Vegan Coconut No-Churn Ice Cream

205 Orange and White Chocolate No-Churn Ice Cream
  by Chef Seema Pankhania

206 Chocolate Milkshakes
  Malted Chocolate Milkshakes
  Chocolate–Peanut Butter Milkshakes

208 Strawberry Shortcake Icebox Bars

211 Kulfi Lollies

212 Root Beer Floats
  Creamsicle Floats

Kiwi-Berry Frozen Lemonade Lollies

MAKES 6 LOLLIES

A little extra sugar in the lemonade base makes sure these ice lollies don't become too icy. If you don't have ice-lolly moulds, you can use six 85 g paper cups instead: Fill the cups, cover the top of each cup with a piece of aluminium foil, and use a paring knife to make a small slit in the middle of the foil. Insert a wooden ice-lolly stick through each slit into the lemonade mixture so the stick is standing straight up.

INGREDIENTS

1 kiwi

325 ml water

75 ml fresh lemon juice (see page 12)

110 g granulated sugar

70 g fresh blueberries, blackberries, or raspberries

!!1. Lay the kiwi on its side on a **chopping board**. Use a **chef's knife** to slice off each end and discard. Use a **vegetable peeler** to peel off all of the skin in strips, going from end to end. Lay the peeled kiwi back on its side and cut it crossways into six 5 mm (¼ in) thick slices. Set aside.

2. In a **small saucepan**, combine the water, lemon juice, and sugar. Place over medium heat and cook, stirring occasionally with a **wooden spoon**, until the mixture comes to a simmer (small bubbles appear all over the surface) and the sugar dissolves, 4 to 6 minutes. Turn off the hob and slide the saucepan to a cool part of the hob. Let cool to room temperature, about 15 minutes.

3. Meanwhile, divide the kiwi and berries among **six 85 g ice-lolly moulds**.

4. When the lemonade mixture has cooled, transfer it to a **measuring jug** or **medium bowl with a spout**. Pour it over the fruit in each ice-lolly mould. Be sure to leave a little room as the liquid will expand as it freezes. Wiggle the mould a bit to release any trapped air bubbles, then insert the ice-lolly sticks.

5. Place the ice lollies in the freezer until frozen solid, 5 to 6 hours. To serve, select a **bowl** large enough to hold your ice-lolly moulds and fill it with warm water. Dip the moulds into the warm water, covering only the sides, for 10 to 30 seconds, then lift the moulds out of the water and gently pull out the lollies. Enjoy immediately!

Apricot-Berry Frozen Lemonade Lollies

Use 1 apricot, stoned and cut into twelve 5 mm (¼ in) thick slices, in place of the kiwi.

 **FUN FOOD FACT**

Clara Barton was a nurse during the US Civil War and the founder of the American Red Cross. But she was suspicious of drinks like lemonade. She believed that drinking cold drinks could "reduce the temperature of the stomach, thereby disrupting digestion, and for this reason should be avoided during or immediately after meals".

MAKES ABOUT 1 LITRE

Vanilla No-Churn Ice Cream

INGREDIENTS

400 g tin sweetened condensed milk

120 ml buttermilk

1 tablespoon vanilla extract

¼ teaspoon table salt

1 recipe Whipped Cream (page 17), or canned whipped cream

60–85 g crushed cookies, sweets, and/or other mix-in (optional)

You can keep this vanilla ice cream simple (classic!), or you can get creative with optional mix-ins. You might stir in crushed Oreos or other biscuits, or add M&M's or chopped-up chocolate bars. You can even swirl in some caramel, fudge sauce, or jam. It's also fine to mix and match, sticking with a total of about 60–85 g mix-ins. Just avoid fresh fruit and berries, as they will turn icy in the freezer.

1. Place a 23 by 13 cm (9 by 5 in) metal loaf tin in the freezer to chill. In a large bowl, whisk together the sweetened condensed milk, buttermilk, vanilla, and salt.

2. If you're making the whipped cream, whip the cream to soft peaks. Add about one-third of the whipped cream to the bowl with the sweetened condensed milk mixture. Using a rubber spatula, stir gently until well mixed.

3. Add the remaining whipped cream on top. Using the spatula, cut downwards through the mixture to the bottom of the bowl, then scrape along the bottom and up the side closest to you, scooping the mixture from the bottom and folding it over the top. Rotate the bowl a quarter turn and repeat, cutting downwards, scraping along the bottom and up the side, and folding over the top. Continue until the mixture is just combined but the whipped cream is still fluffy. If using one or more mix-ins, add and stir gently just until evenly distributed.

4. Use the spatula to scrape the mixture into the chilled loaf tin and smooth it into an even layer. Cover the pan with cling film and place in the freezer until frozen solid, about 6 hours. Scoop and serve.

MINT CHOCOLATE CHIP NO-CHURN ICE CREAM

Swap out the vanilla extract for 1 teaspoon peppermint extract. For the mix-in, gently stir in 90 g mini chocolate chips at the end of step 3.

French author Louise d'Alq published an etiquette guide in 1883 that explained how the dessert course should be served. Cheese should come first, then fruit, cakes, and "confectionary". Ice cream should be last.

VEGAN COCONUT NO-CHURN ICE CREAM

MAKES ABOUT 1 LITRE

INGREDIENTS

25 g sweetened coconut flakes

2 (400 g) tins full-fat coconut milk, chilled

350 g tin evaporated coconut milk, chilled

1 teaspoon vanilla extract

Coconut milk is a wonderful alternative to dairy milk when it comes to making ice cream. Chilling the coconut milk in the fridge for at least 3 hours or up to overnight helps bring the coconut cream to the top of the tin. Save the lighter coconut milk that's left over after draining the coconut cream for smoothies or porridge.

!! 1. Place a **23 by 13 cm (9 by 5 in) metal loaf tin** in the freezer. Spread the coconut flakes into an even layer on a **small microwave-safe plate**. Microwave at 100 per cent power for 30 seconds. Use a **rubber spatula** to stir the flakes. Return the plate to the microwave and continue heating in 30-second increments, stirring after each increment, until the flakes are light golden brown, about 2 minutes. Using **oven gloves**, remove the plate from the microwave and set aside.

2. Place a **fine-mesh sieve** over a **medium bowl**. Pour the coconut milk into the sieve, capturing the coconut cream solids in the sieve and the liquid in the bowl. Reserve the liquid for another use.

3. Add the coconut cream solids to the bowl of a **stand mixer** fitted with the **whisk attachment** or to a **large bowl** if you're using a **handheld mixer**. Whip on medium-high speed until soft peaks form (see page 17), about 3 minutes. Stop the mixer.

4. Add the evaporated coconut milk and vanilla to the bowl. Continue to whip at medium-high speed until the mixture has begun to thicken and fluff up slightly (it should be about the consistency of pancake batter), about 3 minutes.

5. Transfer the coconut mixture to the chilled loaf tin. Sprinkle the toasted coconut flakes over the top.

6. Cover the loaf tin with **cling film** and place in the freezer until frozen solid, at least 6 hours or up to overnight.

7. When ready to serve, remove the ice cream from the freezer and set on a worktop to soften for 5 to 10 minutes before scooping.

FUN FOOD FACT

Until Nancy Johnson came around, ice cream was a luxury. It took a lot of effort and a lot of time to make each batch. But in 1843, she patented the "Artificial Freezer", the first hand-cranked ice cream freezer, and set off an ice cream revolution!

YOU'RE THE CHEF!

"It was so awesome and good! My family LOVED it. It tasted exactly like vanilla ice cream except I got to add in my favourite sweets! So good and so easy. I would definitely make again and recommend." —Lux, 13

A certain kind of tea always makes Seema think of weekends at her family home. On Sunday mornings, Seema's mum would make masala chai, a sweet spiced Indian tea, for everyone in the family. Then they would have a big breakfast together.

Seema's first kitchen gadget was a mortar and pestle. At six or seven years old, she would report for kitchen duty. While her mum chopped and prepped the ingredients for dinner, Seema would pound ginger, garlic, and chillies into flavourful pastes for her family's curries.

By 13, she had graduated to making elaborate cakes for her friends — one in the shape of the earth, another built to look like an exploding volcano.

In college, she stumbled on a nearby Asian supermarket. With her limited student budget and boundless curiosity, she bought some unfamiliar ingredients and began to research and experiment. What could she make with this Korean chilli paste called gochujang? How could she use dried shrimp paste? She realized how little she really knew about cooking — and unlocked a desire to learn more. After working at a few restaurants, she began creating content online. In one TikTok series, she challenged herself to make the national dishes of countries all over the world, from a Moroccan tagine and Greek moussaka to Malaysian nasi lemak.

Cooking has always come easy to her, but reading and writing were more difficult. Seema is dyslexic. Because of her learning disability, she never dreamed she would be able to publish a book. But she's done it, and she's incredibly proud of *Craveable*, her collection of recipes that encourages everyone to have fun in the kitchen.

As a young person, Seema didn't like the taste of coffee or mushrooms. Now they are some of her favourite flavours. It's good to remember that your taste buds change and develop as you grow up, so even if you don't like something today, you can try it again in the future.

Orange and White Chocolate No-Churn Ice Cream

SERVES 6

"The flavours of this ice cream are inspired by an incredible ice cream I had during a trip to the Isle of Man. A very cute couple who owned the local ice cream shop encouraged me to try a scoop of their orange and white chocolate, and although I'm not usually a big fan of white chocolate, the two flavours together were unbelievable." —Seema Pankhania

Ingredients

- 130 g white chocolate chips or small chunks of a white chocolate bar
- 150 ml sweetened condensed milk
- Pinch of table salt
- 1 large orange, cut in half
- 535 ml double cream

1. Put the chocolate into a large microwave-safe bowl. Microwave at 50 per cent power for 30 seconds. Remove the bowl and stir with a silicone spatula. Pop the bowl back into the microwave and repeat warming at 50 per cent power for 30 seconds and then stirring until the white chocolate has melted, about 2 minutes total.

2. Add the condensed milk and salt to the melted chocolate.

3. Squeeze the juice from half of the orange (see page 12). You should have about 60 ml. Add the juice to the bowl. Save the other half of the orange as a snack for later. Whisk the ingredients together until combined.

4. Whip the cream to stiff peaks (see page 17). Add about one-third of the whipped cream to the bowl with the white chocolate mixture. Use the silicone spatula to gently stir it together until well combined.

5. Add the remaining whipped cream on top. Cut downwards through the mixture with the spatula to the bottom of the bowl, then scrape along the side and fold over from the bottom to the top. Rotate the bowl a quarter turn and cut, scrape, and fold over again. Continue until the mixture is just combined, but the whipped cream is still fluffy. Transfer the mixture to an airtight 2 litre container, place in the freezer, and freeze overnight.

6. When ready to serve, remove the ice cream from the freezer. Scoop into bowls and enjoy!

If Seema could give her younger self some advice, she would say, "There are no expectations or pressure. You can cook whatever you like however you like. If it goes wrong, it's fine! You just learn from the mistakes and make it better next time."

FROZEN TREATS

SERVES 2

CHOCOLATE MILKSHAKES

INGREDIENTS

500 g chocolate ice cream

120 ml whole milk

60 ml chocolate syrup, plus more for serving (optional)

Pinch of table salt

Whipped cream, sprinkles, and/or maraschino cherries for serving (optional)

We loved the double chocolate flavour of using chocolate ice cream and chocolate syrup in these milkshakes, but you can swap in vanilla ice cream instead if that's what you've got. The chocolate syrup will give the milkshakes a mild but still chocolatey flavour. For a classic diner-style treat, top your milkshakes with whipped cream (use ½ recipe Whipped Cream from page 17, or use shop-bought whipped topping), sprinkles, and/or maraschino cherries.

1. Remove the ice cream from the freezer and set it on a worktop until soft, about 10 minutes. (The container should give a little bit when you squeeze the sides, but the ice cream shouldn't be completely melted.)

2. Meanwhile, place **two tall drinking glasses** in the refrigerator or freezer to chill.

3. Add the milk, chocolate syrup, and salt to a **blender**, then use a **rubber spatula** to scoop the softened ice cream on top. Place the lid on the blender and hold it in place with a **folded kitchen towel**. Blend the mixture until smooth, about 30 seconds.

4. Remove the glasses from the fridge or freezer. If you like, drizzle some extra chocolate sauce down the insides of the chilled glasses. Divide the milkshake mixture evenly between the two glasses. Add the toppings, if desired, and serve immediately.

MALTED CHOCOLATE MILKSHAKES

Add 2 tablespoons malted milk powder to the blender along with the milk and other ingredients in step 3.

CHOCOLATE-PEANUT BUTTER MILKSHAKES

Add 1 tablespoon smooth peanut butter to the blender along with the milk and other ingredients in step 3.

FUN FOOD FACT

In 2013, Jelena Pasic opened the neighbourhood diner Harlem Shake to celebrate the unique history and vibe of Harlem, New York City. Its best-selling milkshake is red velvet flavoured.

MAKES 12 BARS

STRAWBERRY SHORTCAKE ICEBOX BARS

INGREDIENTS

275 g shortbread biscuits

14 g freeze-dried strawberries

¼ teaspoon table salt

60 g unsalted butter, melted and cooled (see page 11)

315 g strawberry jam

1 litre strawberry ice cream

You might be thinking: What? Strawberry shortcakes twice in the same book?! While the ones in chapter 3 are a take on the more traditional dessert, these icebox bars are inspired by the ice lollies sold by neighbourhood ice cream vans. Freeze-dried strawberries help intensify the strawberry flavour while also making the topping look like fun confetti. Feel free to use vanilla ice cream instead of strawberry as well!

1. Fit an **20 cm (8 in) square metal baking tin** with a **parchment paper** sling (see page 13).

2. Put around 140 g of the shortbread biscuits and all of the freeze-dried strawberries into a **large sealable plastic bag**, press out all of the air, and seal the bag. Lay the bag flat on a worktop and use a **rolling pin** or the bottom of a **small saucepan** to crush the biscuits and berries into crumbs. This is the crumb topping. Transfer it to a **medium bowl**.

3. Add the remaining shortbread biscuits and salt to a **food processor** and lock the lid into place. Pulse until the cookies are the texture of sand, about fifteen 1-second pulses.

4. Remove the processor lid, add the melted butter, and lock the lid back into place. Pulse until the crumbs are moistened and the mixture looks like wet sand, about ten 1-second pulses.

!!5. Remove the processor lid and carefully remove the processor blade. Use a **rubber spatula** to transfer the crumb mixture to the parchment-lined baking tin. Use the bottom of a **dry mug or glass** to press the crumb mixture into an even layer on the bottom of the tin.

6. Pour the jam onto the crumb crust and use the spatula to spread it into an even layer. Place the baking tin in the freezer for 20 minutes. Remove the ice cream from the freezer and place on a worktop to soften while the crust is freezing.

YOU'RE THE CHEF!
"They were really, really good! It tasted like a strawberry-frosted cookie but better! It also looked really pretty!" —Nicolina, 11

7 When the crust has set, use an **ice cream scoop** to scoop the softened ice cream into the baking tin. Cover the dish with **cling film**. Use your hands to gently push the ice cream into an even layer. Remove the cling film and discard.

8 Working quickly, sprinkle the reserved crumb topping in an even layer on top of the ice cream.

9 Cover the tin with a piece of clean cling film and place in the freezer to chill until firm, at least 3 hours or up to 1 week.

!! 10 To serve, hold a **butter knife** under warm water for about 30 seconds, then run it along the edges of the tin to release the slab. Holding the edges of the parchment sling, carefully lift the slab out of the baking tin and onto a **chopping board**. Leave to soften for 10 minutes. Use a **chef's knife** to cut the slab into thirds in one direction, then cut it into quarters in the other direction. Serve right away.

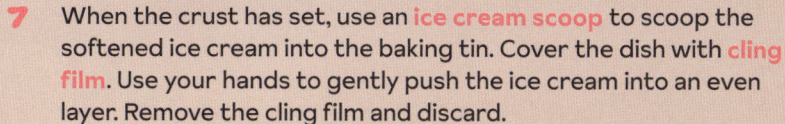

Kulfi Lollies

MAKES 6 LOLLIES

Kulfi is a sweet and creamy dessert popular in India and Pakistan. It's similar to ice cream but is made with milk, while ice cream often includes milk and cream. For traditional kulfi, whole milk is simmered for hours until it's thick and sweet. This recipe makes things much quicker by using sweetened condensed milk and milk powder along with liquid whole milk. If you don't have ice-lolly moulds, you can use six 85 g paper cups instead: Fill the cups, cover the top of each cup with a piece of aluminium foil, and use a paring knife to make a small slit in the middle of the foil. Insert a wooden ice-lolly stick through each slit into the kulfi mixture so the stick is standing straight up.

INGREDIENTS

600 ml whole milk

150 ml sweetened condensed milk

45 g non-fat dry milk powder

1 tablespoon granulated sugar

1 teaspoon green cardamom pods (about 12 pods)

Pinch of saffron threads (optional)

Finely chopped pistachios, for sprinkling (optional)

1. In a **large saucepan**, **whisk** together the whole milk, sweetened condensed milk, milk powder, and sugar. Add the cardamom pods and saffron (if using). Place over medium heat and cook, stirring occasionally with a **wooden spoon**, until the mixture comes to a simmer (small bubbles appear all over the surface) and the sugar dissolves, 8 to 10 minutes.

2. Lower the heat to medium-low and continue to cook, stirring and scraping the bottom of the saucepan often with the wooden spoon, until the mixture thickens slightly, about 10 minutes.

3. Turn off the hob and slide the saucepan to a cool part of the hob. Let cool to room temperature, about 30 minutes.

4. Use a **spoon** to scoop out the cardamom pods and discard. (If the milk mixture formed a skin on top as it cooled, that's OK. Just stir or **whisk** it back into the rest of the mixture.) Transfer the cooled milk mixture to a **measuring jug** or **medium bowl with a spout**.

5. Divide the milk mixture evenly among **six 85 g ice-lolly moulds**. Be sure to leave a little room at the top of each mould, as the liquid will expand as it freezes. Insert the ice-lolly sticks.

6. Place the kulfi lollies in the freezer until they're frozen solid, 5 to 6 hours. To unmould the ice lollies for serving, fill a **large bowl** with warm water. Dip the moulds into the warm water, covering only the sides, for 10 to 30 seconds, then lift the moulds out of the water and gently pull out the lollies. Sprinkle each lolly with pistachios (if using) and enjoy immediately.

 FUN FOOD FACT

Padma Lakshmi is a model and food expert and the host and a producer of the US TV show *Top Chef*. As a child growing up in Madras (now Chennai), India, she and her grandfather shared a love of food. She would sometimes sneak to the local shop to buy ice cream for her grandfather (who wasn't supposed to have sugar). Their secret sweets soirees came to an end when her grandmother caught them.

FROZEN TREATS

SERVES 2

ROOT BEER FLOATS

Root beer floats have been around in the USA since the late 1800s! This refreshing treat comes together in just a few minutes.

INGREDIENTS

2 scoops vanilla ice cream, measured separately

340 ml root beer

½ recipe Whipped Cream (page 17), or canned whipped cream

1 Have ready **two small drinking glasses**. Use an **ice cream scoop** to add 1 scoop of ice cream to each glass.

2 Slowly pour half of the root beer into each glass.

3 Top with whipped cream (if using). Serve each float with a **straw**.

CREAMSICLE FLOATS

Substitute orange soda for the root beer to make a creamsicle float.

FUN FOOD FACT

Emmy award–winning actor Zendaya loves ice cream. One of her favourite flavours? Brown sugar almond brittle.

ACKNOWLEDGEMENTS

Rebel Girls would like to acknowledge all the chefs who contributed recipes! Thank you for sharing your stories, memories, and recipes with us.

Abi Balingit	Chrissy Tracey	Joanne Chang	Nadiya Hussain	Seema Pankhania
Alana Kysar	Deb Perelman	Luisa Weiss	Rachel Gurjar	Vallery Lomas
Aran Goyoaga	Jennifer Latham	Molly Yeh	Reem Assil	

Thank you to the wonderful models who brought their energy and bright smiles to the photo shoot for this book.

Avi	Haven	Keira H.	Londyn	Sophie
Boston	Ina	Keira M.	Noor	Zayna
Camila	Julianna	Laila	Parker	Zoe

Rebel Girls would like to acknowledge all the Rebels who helped us test these recipes — and their families too! Thank you for sharing your thoughts about food and your kitchen adventures with us.

Addy	Caroline R.	Emily O.	Liliya	Nova A.
Aida	Cecilia	Emme	Lilly	Nova M.
Alejandra	Charley S.	Emmi	Lily	Olivia C.
Ali	Charley S.	Estela	Luka	Olivia W.
Alice	Charlotte	Evelyn	Lux	Penny
Alisiya	Claire	Evie P.	Lyra	Place
Alison	Clara	Evie S.	Maddie G.	Remi
Althea	Colleen	Evy	Maddie S.	Rena
Amelie	Coralie	Ezra	Madeleine	Robyn
Annabelle	Dalia	Fiona	Madeline	Sabine
Arden	Dalise	Goldie	Mali	Sagan
Autumn M.	Éabha	Hannah	Maren	Saige
Autumn O.	Elettra	Hayley	Maria	Savannah
Autumn S.	Elizabeth	Heather	Marian	Sibella
Autumn S.	Ella	Isabelle	May	Sophia P.
Ava P.	Ella S.	Jolene	Maya	Sophia S.
Ava P.	Ella S.	Kate	Maya P.	Sydney F.
Ava T.	Ella T.	Keira	Mia	Sydney S.
Blake	Ellen	Keya	Miriam	Tula
Bowie	Ellia	Kira	Monroe	Violet
Bridget	Eloise	Laura	Naoise	Viva
Cali	Elsa C.	Layla	Neva	The Wild Ginger
Camille	Elsa N.	Leanor	Nicolina	Willa
Caroline H.	Emily C.	Leila Élodie	Nina	Zaida

And finally, special thanks to the Rebel Girls team: Amy Pfister, Anjelika Temple, Annie Liu, Denise Gomez-Rivera, Erika Harvey, Haley Dapkus, Isadora Manzaro, Jes Wolfe, Joy Smith, Michon Vanderpoel, Rachel Toby, and Sarah Parvis.

About Rebel Girls

Rebel Girls, a certified B Corporation, is a global, multi-platform empowerment brand dedicated to helping raise the most inspired and confident generation of girls. The brand purposefully creates content, products, and experiences to empower Generation Alpha girls and equip them with the knowledge and tools they need to thrive. Because confident girls will radically transform the world.

With a growing community of 40 million self-identified Rebel Girls spanning more than 115 countries, the brand engages with Gen Alpha through its book series, premier app, events, and merchandise. To date, Rebel Girls has sold more than 11 million books in 62 languages and reached 85 million digital listens/views. Award recognition includes the *New York Times* bestseller list, 2022 Apple Design Award for Social Impact, 10 Webby Awards, and more.

Join the Rebel Girls Community!

Head to rebelgirls.com and join our email list for exclusive sneak peeks, new content drops, creative activities, and more. If you want to say hi or have any questions, email us at hello@rebelgirls.com. We love hearing from you!

More Places to Find Us!

Watch: youtube.com/RebelGirls

Listen: rebelgirls.com/audio

Shop: rebelgirls.com/shop

And for your daily dose of Rebel Girls, be sure to follow us on Instagram and Facebook: @rebelgirls

If you could share a meal with any woman working today or from the past, who would you choose?

Meet More Rebels!

Download the Rebel Girls App to hear hundreds of stories about extraordinary women and girls from around the world and throughout history.

MORE FROM REBEL GIRLS!

Let stories about real-life women and girls entertain and inspire you.

Enjoy interactive books and gifts!

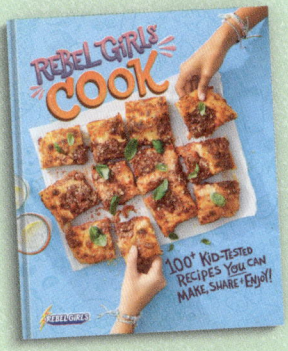

Boost your kitchen confidence, impress your family, and enjoy 100+ awesome kid-tested recipes with *Rebel Girls Cook*.

Find helpful advice and Q&As between tweens and experts in the Growing Up Powerful series.

Read letters, poems, essays, and more from 145 extraordinary teens and women.

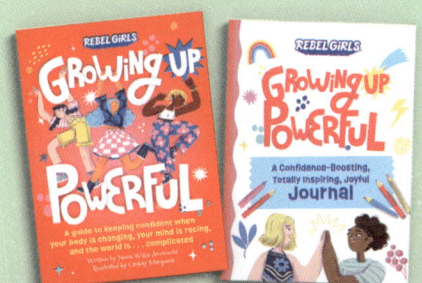

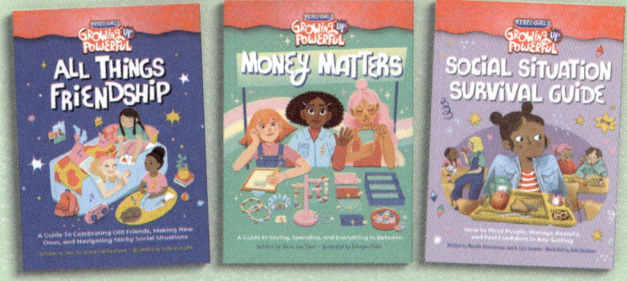

Dig deeper into the lives of five real-life heroines with the Rebel Girls chapter book series.

 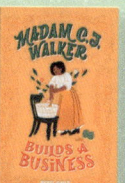 

 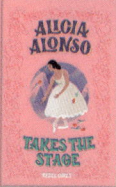

Go on an incredible middle-grade adventure with *Nina and the Mysterious Mailbox*.

INDEX

Note: Page references in *italics* indicate photographs.

A
d'Alq, Louise, 198
Alleyne, Yonette, 180
Almond Butter
   –Miso Cookies with Chocolate Chunks, *40*, 41
   Stuffed Dates, 140, *141*
Almonds
   Lebanese-Style Fruit Cocktail, *130*, 131
Apple(s)
   how to peel, core, and cut, 156
   Pastries, Upside-Down, *144*, 145
   Pie, Dutch, 154, *155*
Apricot
   -Berry Frozen Lemonade Lollies, 197
   Hamantaschen, 51–55, *53*
Artemis, 24
Assil, Reem, 129
Avocados
   Lebanese-Style Fruit Cocktail, *130*, 131

B
Baking tin foil or parchment sling, 13
Balingit, Abi, 160
Banana(s)
   Capirotada de Agua, *164*, 165–66
   Pudding, 167–68, *169*
   Split Bites, *138*, 139
Bars
   Brookies, 66, *67*
   Cereal Treats Your Way, 64, *65*
   Granola, Choose-Your-Own-Adventure, 46–47, *47*
   Lemon, 42–43, *43*
   Raspberry Crumb, 29–31, *30*
   Salted Caramel Chocolate Brownie Bites, 58–59, *59*
   Salted Chocolate-Filled Brownie Bites, 59
   Strawberry Shortcake Icebox, 208–9, *209*
   toothpick test for doneness, 12
Barton, Clara, 197
Berry(ies). *See also specific berries*
   Any-, Cobbler, 124
   -Apricot Frozen Lemonade Lollies, 197
   -Kiwi Frozen Lemonade Lollies, *196*, 197
   Lebanese-Style Fruit Cocktail, *130*, 131

Blackberry Cobbler, *122*, 123–24
Blueberries
   Any-Berry Cobbler, 124
   Apricot-Berry Frozen Lemonade Lollies, 197
   Kiwi-Berry Frozen Lemonade Lollies, *196*, 197
Bolo de Cenoura, 80–82, *81*
Bread pudding. *See* Capirotada
Brookies, 66, *67*
Brown Butter Oatmeal Cookies, 35–36, *36*
Brownie Bites
   Salted Caramel Chocolate, 58–59, *59*
   Salted Chocolate-Filled, 59
Butter
   bringing to room temperature, 11
   Brown, Oatmeal Cookies, 35–36, *36*
   melting, 11
   softening, 11
Buttercream
   Confetti, 75
   Vanilla, 75

C
Cake tins
   lining bottom with parchment, 14
   removing cake from, 15
Cakes
   Basic (in a Blender), 77–79, *78*
   Bolo de Cenoura, 80–82, *81*
   Chocoflan, 170–72, *171*
   Chocolate, Flourless, 104, *105*
   Chocolate–Peanut Butter Mug, 90, *91*
   Coffee Crumb, 114–16, *115*
   Confetti Sheet Cake, *70*, 71
   Courgette Spice, One-Bowl, *88*, 89
   Lemon–Poppy Seed Pound, 93
   Lemon Pound, 92–93, *93*
   No-Bake Cheesecake with Any-Cookie Crust, 117–18, *119*
   Orange Semolina, 98–99, *99*
   Pastel de Tres Leches, 112
   Pear and Cardamom Loaf, 101–3, *102*
   removing from cake tin, 15
   Strawberry Snacking, 95–97, *96*
   toothpick test for doneness, 12
   Tres Leches de Coco, 110–12, *113*
   Victoria Sponge, 83–84, *85*

Capirotada de Agua, *164*, 165–66
Caramel, Salted, Chocolate Brownie Bites, 58–59, *59*
Cardamom
　Kulfi Lollies, *210*, 211
　and Pear Loaf Cake, 101–3, *102*
　Stuffed Dates, 140, *141*
Carrots
　Bolo de Cenoura, 80–82, *81*
Cereal Treats Your Way, 64, *65*
Chang, Joanne, 60
Chattopadhyay, Kamaladevi, 59
Cheese. *See also* Cream Cheese
　Capirotada de Agua, *164*, 165–66
Cheesecake, No-Bake, with Any-Cookie Crust, 117–18, *119*
Cherry(ies)
　Banana Split Bites, *138*, 139
　Chocolate Galette, 174
　Galette, 173–74, *175*
Chocoflan, 170–72, *171*
Chocolate
　Banana Split Bites, *138*, 139
　Brookies, 66, *67*
　Brownie Bites, Salted Caramel, 58–59, *59*
　Cake, Flourless, 104, *105*
　Chip Mint No-Churn Ice Cream, 198
　Chip Mochi Muffins, *108*, 109
　Chocoflan, 170–72, *171*
　Chunks, Almond Butter–Miso Cookies with, 40, *41*
　Galette, Cherry, 174
　Glaze, 80–82, *81*
　Homemade Oreos, 61–63, *62*
　Hot Cocoa Cookies, 56–57, *57*
　Icing, 77–79, *78*
　Milkshakes, 206, *207*
　Milkshakes, Malted, 206
　Peanut Blossom Cookies, *48*, 49–50
　–Peanut Butter Milkshakes, 206
　–Peanut Butter Mug Cake, 90, *91*
　Pudding, Oat Milk, 186, *187*
　Salted, -Filled Brownie Bites, 59
　Tahini Blossom Cookies, 50
　Tarte Soleil with Dulce de Leche Dipping Sauce, *190*, 191–93
　White, and Orange No-Churn Ice Cream, *204*, 205
Cinnamon
　Coffee Crumb Cake, 114–16, *115*
　Gingerbread Cookies, 32–34, *33*
　Melomakarona, *22*, 23–24
　One-Bowl Courgette Spice Cake, *88*, 89
　Pastel de Tres Leches, 112
Citrus. *See also specific citrus fruits*
　juicing, 12
　Sugar Cookies, Chewy, 21
　zesting, 12
Cleopatra, 141
Cobbler
　Any-Berry, 124
　Blackberry, *122*, 123–24
Cocoa powder, dusting with, 16
Coconut
　No-Churn Ice Cream, Vegan, 199, *201*
　Pastel de Tres Leches, 112
　Stuffed Dates, 140, *141*
　Tres Leches de Coco, 110–12, *113*
Coffee Crumb Cake, 114–16, *115*
Confetti Buttercream, 75
Confetti Sheet Cake, *70*, 71
Cookie, Any, Crust, No-Bake Cheesecake with, 117–18, *119*
Cookies
　Almond Butter–Miso, with Chocolate Chunks, 40, *41*
　Brown Butter Oatmeal, 35–36, *36*
　Chewy Candy Sugar, 21, *21*
　Chewy Citrus Sugar, 21
　Chewy Sugar, 20–21, *21*
　Gingerbread, 32–34, *33*
　Hamantaschen, 51–55, *53*
　Homemade Oreos, 61–63, *62*
　Hot Cocoa, 56–57, *57*
　Melomakarona, *22*, 23–24
　Peanut Blossom, *48*, 49–50
　Shortbread, 25–26, *27*
　Tahini Blossom, 50
Courgette Spice Cake, One-Bowl, *88*, 89
Couscous
　Thiakry, 182, *183*
Cream, whipping, 17
Cream Cheese
　Chocoflan, 170–72, *171*

Cream cheese, *continued*
   Frosting, 73, 74
   Guava and Cheese Pastelitos, *184*, 185
   No-Bake Cheesecake with Any-Cookie Crust, 117–18, *119*
   No-Bake Key Lime Pie Jars, 146, *147*
   One-Bowl Courgette Spice Cake, *88*, 89
   softening, 11
Creamsicle Floats, 212
Crêpes Suzette, 134–35, *135*
Crispy rice cereal
   Cereal Treats Your Way, 64, *65*
Crumble, 116
Cupcakes
   Chocolate Chip Mochi Muffins, *108*, 109
Cupcakes, Red Velvet, 72, *73*

D
Dates, Stuffed, 140, *141*
Day, Mildred, 64
Digestive biscuit crumbs
   No-Bake Key Lime Pie Jars, 146, *147*
Dulce de Leche Dipping Sauce, Chocolate Tarte Soleil with, *190*, 191–93
Dutch Apple Pie, 154, *155*

E
Eggs
   bringing to room temperature, 11
   separating yolks and whites, 37
Elena, Princess of Montenegro, 104
Elizabeth II, Queen of England, 158
Elliott, Mabel Beatrice, 43

F
Floats
   Creamsicle, 212
   Root Beer, 212, *213*
Flourless Chocolate Cake, 104, *105*
Foil slings, creating, 13
Fool
   Raspberry, 158, *159*
   Rhubarb, 159
Frozen desserts
   Apricot-Berry Frozen Lemonade Pops, 197
   Chocolate Milkshakes, 206, *207*
   Chocolate–Peanut Butter Milkshakes, 206
   Creamsicle Floats, 212
   Kiwi-Berry Frozen Lemonade Lollies, *196*, 197
   Kulfi Lollies, *210*, 211
   Malted Chocolate Milkshakes, 206
   Mint Chocolate Chip No-Churn Ice Cream, 198
   Orange and White Chocolate No-Churn Ice Cream, *204*, 205
   Root Beer Floats, 212, *213*
   Strawberry Shortcake Icebox Bars, 208–9, *209*
   Vanilla No-Churn Ice Cream, 198, *200*
   Vegan Coconut No-Churn Ice Cream, 199, *201*
Fruit. *See also specific fruits*
   Choose-Your-Own-Adventure Granola Bars, 46–47, *47*
   Cocktail, Lebanese-Style, *130*, 131
Fruit desserts
   Any-Berry Cobbler, 124
   Banana Split Bites, *138*, 139
   Blackberry Cobbler, *122*, 123–24
   Crêpes Suzette, 134–35, *135*
   Lebanese-Style Fruit Cocktail, *130*, 131
   Peach Melba, 132, *133*
   Strawberry Shortcakes, 126, *127*
   Stuffed Dates, 140, *141*

G
Galettes
   Cherry, 173–74, *175*
   Cherry Chocolate, 174
Gilmore, Georgia, 93
Ginger
   Gingerbread Cookies, 32–34, *33*
   One-Bowl Courgette Spice Cake, *88*, 89
Glaze, Chocolate, 80–82, *81*
Goyoaga, Aran, 39
Granola Bars, Choose-Your-Own-Adventure, 46–47, *47*
Guava and Cheese Pastelitos, *184*, 185
Gurjar, Rachel, 94
Guyanese Pine Tarts, *178*, 179–81

H
Hamantaschen, 51–55, *53*
Heatter, Maida, 147
Honey
   in Ancient Greece, 24
   Melomakarona, *22*, 23–24
   Stuffed Dates, 140, *141*
Hot Cocoa Cookies, 56–57, *57*
Hussain, Nadiya, 100

I
Icebox Bars, Strawberry Shortcake, 208–9, *209*
Ice Cream
   Chocolate Milkshakes, 206, *207*

Chocolate–Peanut Butter
    Milkshakes, 206
Creamsicle Floats, 212
Malted Chocolate Milkshakes, 206
Mint Chocolate Chip No-Churn, 198
Orange and White Chocolate No-Churn,
    204, 205
Peach Melba, 132, *133*
Root Beer Floats, 212, *213*
Strawberry Shortcake Icebox Bars,
    208–9, *209*
Vanilla No-Churn, 198, *200*
Vegan Coconut No-Churn, 199, *201*
Ice lollies. *See* Lollies
Icing
    Chocolate, 77–79, *78*
    Confetti Buttercream, 75
    Cream Cheese, *73*, 74
    Vanilla Buttercream, 75
Icing sugar, dusting with, 16
Inés de la Cruz, Sor Juana, 192
Ingredients, measuring, 10–11

J
Jensen, Malitta, 64
Johnson, Nancy, 199

K
Kahlo, Frida, 112
Key Lime Pie Jars, No-Bake, 146, *147*
Kitchen basics, 10–17
Kiwi
    -Berry Frozen Lemonade Lollies,
        196, 197
    Lebanese-Style Fruit Cocktail, *130*, 131
Kulfi Lollies, *210*, 211
Kysar, Alana, 107

L
Lakshmi, Padma, 211
Latham, Jennifer, 76
Lebanese-Style Fruit Cocktail, *130*, 131
Lemon(s)
    Apricot-Berry Frozen Lemonade
        Lollies, 197
    Bars, 42–43, *43*
    juicing, 12
    Kiwi-Berry Frozen Lemonade Lollies,
        196, 197
    –Poppy Seed Pound Cake, 93
    Possets, 176, *177*
    Pound Cake, 92–93, *93*
    zesting, 12
Lewis, Edna, 124

Lime(s)
    juicing, 12
    Key, Pie Jars, No-Bake, 146, *147*
    zesting, 12
Lindgren, Thérése, 71
Lloyd, Bobbie, 168
Loeb, Lisa, 174
Lollies
    Apricot-Berry Frozen Lemonade, 197
    Kiwi-Berry Frozen Lemonade, *196*, 197
    Kulfi, *210*, 211
Lomas, Vallery, 87
Lorde, Audre, 152
Low, Juliette Gordon, 20

M
Malted Chocolate Milkshakes, 206
Mango
    Cream Pie, 161–63, *162*
    Lebanese-Style Fruit Cocktail, *130*, 131
    Sago, 188, *189*
Margaret, Princess, 158
Marshmallows
    Cereal Treats Your Way, 64, *65*
    Hot Cocoa Cookies, 56–57, *57*
Mary, Queen of Scots, 26
Measuring jugs, 10
Measuring spoons, 11
Melomakarona, *22*, 23–24
Milk, bringing to room temperature, 11
Milkshakes
    Chocolate, 206, *207*
    Chocolate–Peanut Butter, 206
    Malted Chocolate, 206
Millet
    Thiakry, 182, *183*
Mint Chocolate Chip No-Churn Ice
    Cream, 198
Mochi Chocolate Chip Muffins, *108*, 109
Morrison, Susan, 34
Moxley, Pamela, 73
Moxon, Elizabeth, 176
Muffins, Chocolate Chip Mochi,
    108, 109
Mug Cake, Chocolate–Peanut Butter,
    90, *91*

N
Nilla Wafer cookies
    Banana Pudding, 167–68, *169*
No-Bake Cheesecake with Any-Cookie
    Crust, 117–18, *119*
No-Bake Key Lime Pie Jars, 146, *147*
No-Churn Ice Cream
    Mint Chocolate Chip, 198

No-Churn Ice Cream, *continued*
  Orange and White Chocolate, *204*, 205
  Vanilla, 198, *200*
  Vegan Coconut, 199, *201*
Nut butter. *See also* Peanut Butter
  Almond Butter–Miso Cookies with Chocolate Chunks, *40*, 41
  Choose-Your-Own-Adventure Granola Bars, 46–47, *47*
  Stuffed Dates, 140, *141*
Nuts
  Brown Butter Oatmeal Cookies, 35–36, *36*
  Choose-Your-Own-Adventure Granola Bars, 46–47, *47*
  Kulfi Lollies, *210*, 211
  Lebanese-Style Fruit Cocktail, *130*, 131
  Melomakarona, *22*, 23–24
  One-Bowl Courgette Spice Cake, *88*, 89
  Stuffed Dates, 140, *141*
  Thiakry, 182, *183*

O
Oat Milk Chocolate Pudding, 186, *187*
Oats
  Brown Butter Oatmeal Cookies, 35–36, *36*
  Choose-Your-Own-Adventure Granola Bars, 46–47, *47*
  One-Bowl Courgette Spice Cake, *88*, 89
Orange(s)
  Creamsicle Floats, 212
  Crêpes Suzette, 134–35, *135*
  juicing, 12
  Melomakarona, *22*, 23–24
  Semolina Cake, 98–99, *99*
  and White Chocolate No-Churn Ice Cream, *204*, 205
  zesting, 12
Oreos, Homemade, 61–63, *62*

P
Pankhania, Seema, 203
Parchment paper
  creating a sling with, 13
  lining cake tin with, 14
Parks, Rosa, 93
Pasic, Jelena, 206
Pastel de Tres Leches, 112
Pastelitos, Guava and Cheese, *184*, 185
Pastries
  Chocolate Tarte Soleil with Dulce de Leche Dipping Sauce, *190*, 191–93
  Guava and Cheese Pastelitos, *184*, 185
  Upside-Down Apple, *144*, 145

Pastry
  rolling out, 153
  shaping into a tart tin, 157
  Sour Cream, 152, *153*
Peach Melba, 132, *133*

Peanut Butter
  –Chocolate Milkshakes, 206
  –Chocolate Mug Cake, 90, *91*
  Peanut Blossom Cookies, *48*, 49–50
Pear and Cardamom Loaf Cake, 101–3, *102*
Pecans
  Brown Butter Oatmeal Cookies, 35–36, *36*
  One-Bowl Courgette Spice Cake, *88*, 89
Perelman, Deb, 28
Pies
  Dutch Apple, 154, *155*
  Mango Cream, 161–63, *162*
Pineapple
  Guyanese Pine Tarts, *178*, 179–81
  Lebanese-Style Fruit Cocktail, *130*, 131
Pistachios
  Kulfi Lollies, *210*, 211
  Stuffed Dates, 140, *141*
Poppy Seed–Lemon Pound Cake, 93
Possets, Lemon, 176, *177*
Pound Cake
  Lemon, 92–93, *93*
  Lemon–Poppy Seed, 93
Price, Rebecca, 74
Profet, Talia, 186
Pudding
  Banana, 167–68, *169*
  Capirotada de Agua, *164*, 165–66
  Lemon Possets, 176, *177*
  Mango Sago, 188, *189*
  No-Bake Key Lime Pie Jars, 146, *147*
  Oat Milk Chocolate, 186, *187*
  Thiakry, 182, *183*
  Vanillepudding mit Erdbeersoße, 149–51, *150*
Puff pastry
  Chocolate Tarte Soleil with Dulce de Leche Dipping Sauce, *190*, 191–93
  Guava and Cheese Pastelitos, *184*, 185
  Upside-Down Apple Pastries, *144*, 145

R
Rain, Patricia, 75
Rainbow sprinkles
  Banana Split Bites, *138*, 139
  Capirotada de Agua, *164*, 165–66
  Confetti Buttercream, 75
  Confetti Sheet Cake, *70*, 71

Raisins
    Capirotada de Agua, *164*, 165–66
    Thiakry, 182, *183*
Raspberry(ies)
    Any-Berry Cobbler, 124
    Apricot-Berry Frozen Lemonade Lollies, 197
    Crumb Bars, 29–31, *30*
    Fool, 158, *159*
    Kiwi-Berry Frozen Lemonade Lollies, *196*, 197
    Peach Melba, 132, *133*
Raspberry jam
    Hamantaschen, 51–55, *53*
    Victoria Sponge, 83–84, *85*
Recipes
    decoding symbols, 9
    getting started, 9
    kitchen basics, 10–17
Red Velvet Cupcakes, 72, *73*
Rhubarb Fool, 159
Rombauer, Irma, 116
Root Beer Floats, 212, *213*

S
Sago, Mango, 188, *189*
Salted Caramel Chocolate Brownie Bites, 58–59, *59*
Salted Chocolate-Filled Brownie Bites, 59
Seed butter
    Choose-Your-Own-Adventure Granola Bars, 46–47, *47*
    Tahini Blossom Cookies, 50
Semolina Orange Cake, 98–99, *99*
Shortbread, 25–26, *27*
Shortcakes, Strawberry, 126, *127*
Smith, Freda, 49
Smith, Maria Ann "Granny", 155
Sour Cream Pastry, 152, *153*
Sow, Mame, 182
Spatulas, 11
Strawberry(ies)
    Any-Berry Cobbler, 124
    Apricot-Berry Frozen Lemonade Lollies, 197
    how to hull, 125
    Kiwi-Berry Frozen Lemonade Lollies, *196*, 197
    Lebanese-Style Fruit Cocktail, *130*, 131
    Shortcake Icebox Bars, 208–9, *209*
    Shortcakes, 126, *127*
    Snacking Cake, 95–97, *96*
    Vanillepudding mit Erdbeersoße, 149–51, *150*
Stuffed Dates, 140, *141*

Sugar Cookies
    Chewy, 20–21, *21*
    Chewy Candy, 21, *21*
    Chewy Citrus, 21
Sweets
    Choose-Your-Own-Adventure Granola Bars, 46–47, *47*
    Sugar Cookies, Chewy, 21, *21*

T
Tahini Blossom Cookies, 50
Tapioca
    Mango Sago, 188, *189*
Tarts. *See also* Galettes
    Chocolate Tarte Soleil with Dulce de Leche Dipping Sauce, *190*, 191–93
    Pine, Guyanese, *178*, 179–81
Thiakry, 182, *183*
Toothpick test, 12
Tosi, Christina, 36
Tracey, Chrissy, 137
Tres Leches, Pastel de, 112
Tres Leches de Coco, 110–12, *113*

U
Upside-Down Apple Pastries, *144*, 145

V
Vanilla
    Buttercream, 75
    No-Churn Ice Cream, 198, *200*
    Vanillepudding mit Erdbeersoße, 149–51, *150*
Vegan Coconut No-Churn Ice Cream, 199, *201*
Victoria Sponge, 83–84, *85*
Villepol, Nitza, 185

W
Walnuts
    Brown Butter Oatmeal Cookies, 35–36, *36*
    Melomakarona, *22*, 23–24
Weiss, Luisa, 148
Whipped cream, preparing, 17
White Chocolate and Orange No-Churn Ice Cream, *204*, 205

Y
Yeh, Molly, 45

Z
Zendaya, 212

Text and illustrations copyright © 2025 by Rebel Girls Inc.
Photographs copyright © 2025 by Jennifer Chong

All rights reserved.

No part of this publication may be reproduced, stored in or introduced into a retrieval system, or transmitted, in any form, or by any means (electronic, mechanical, photocopying, recording, or otherwise), without the prior written permission of the copyright owner.

DK values and supports copyright. Thank you for respecting intellectual property laws by not reproducing, scanning or distributing any part of this publication by any means without permission. By purchasing an authorised edition, you are supporting writers and artists and enabling DK to continue to publish books that inform and inspire readers.

No part of this publication may be used or reproduced in any manner for the purpose of training artificial intelligence technologies or systems. In accordance with Article 4(3) of the DSM Directive 2019/790, DK expressly reserves this work from the text and data mining exception.

First published in Great Britain in 2026 by
Dorling Kindersley Limited
20 Vauxhall Bridge Road,
London SW1V 2SA

The authorised representative in the EEA is
Dorling Kindersley Verlag GmbH. Arnulfstr. 124,
80636 Munich, Germany

FSC™ C018179 — MIX Paper | Supporting responsible forestry

This book was made with Forest Stewardship Council™ certified paper – one small step in DK's commitment to a sustainable future. Learn more at www.dk.com/uk/information/sustainability

Originally published in the United States by Ten Speed Press, an imprint of the Crown Publishing Group, a division of Penguin Random House LLC, New York.
TenSpeed.com

TEN SPEED PRESS and the Ten Speed Press colophon are registered trademarks of Penguin Random House LLC.

Typefaces: Colophon Foundry's Sunset Gothic, Studio Funshop's Goops & Kooky Cloud, Hanoded's Crowd Pleaser, Forth and Wild's Furry Friend

A CIP catalogue record for this book is available from the British Library.
ISBN: 978-0-2417-4018-7

Printed and bound in China

10 9 8 7 6 5 4 3 2 1
001-349452-Jan/26

Acquiring editor: Molly Birnbaum
Project editors: Molly Birnbaum and Gabby Ureña Matos
Production editor: Liana Faughnan
Designer: Annie Marino | Art director: Emma Campion
Production designers: Mari Gill and Faith Hague
Production and pre-press colour: Jane Chinn
Cover lettering: Kristen Brittain
Food stylist: Carrie Ann Purcell
Food stylist assistants: Daniela Swamp and Liza Saragosa
Prop stylist: Hina Mistry | Prop stylist assistant: Jessica Withers
Wardrobe stylist: Emma Campion
Photo assistant: David Koung
Recipe developers: Afton Cyrus and Andrea Rivera Wawrzyn
Chef stories and fun facts: Sarah Parvis
Copy editor: Sharon Silva | Proofreaders: Eldes Tran, Hope Clarke, Sigi Nacson, Tess Rossi, and Miriam Taveras | Indexer: Elizabeth Parson
Publicist: Kristin Casemore | Marketer: Andrea Portanova
UK Editor: Laura Nickoll